PREFACE

1. Scope

This publication provides doctrine for planning, conducting, and assessing military operations in chemical, biological, radiological, or nuclear environments.

2. Purpose

This publication has been prepared under the direction of the Chairman of the Joint Chiefs of Staff (CJCS). It sets forth joint doctrine to govern the activities and performance of the Armed Forces of the United States in joint operations and provides the doctrinal basis for US military coordination with other US Government departments and agencies during operations, and for US military involvement in multinational operations. It provides military guidance for the exercise of authority by combatant commanders and other joint force commanders (JFCs) and prescribes joint doctrine for operations, education, and training. It provides military guidance for use by the Armed Forces in preparing their appropriate plans. It is not the intent of this publication to restrict the authority of the JFC from organizing the force and executing the mission in a manner the JFC deems most appropriate to ensure unity of effort in the accomplishment of the overall objective.

3. Application

a. Joint doctrine established in this publication applies to the Joint Staff, commanders of combatant commands, subunified commands, joint task forces, subordinate components of these commands, Services, and combat support agencies.

b. The guidance in this publication is authoritative; as such, this doctrine will be followed except when, in the judgment of the commander, exceptional circumstances dictate otherwise. If conflicts arise between the contents of this publication and the contents of Service publications, this publication will take precedence unless the CJCS, normally in coordination with the other members of the Joint Chiefs of Staff, has provided more current and specific guidance. Commanders of forces operating as part of a multinational (alliance or coalition) military command should follow multinational doctrine and procedures ratified by the United States. For doctrine and procedures not ratified by the United States, commanders should evaluate and follow the multinational command's doctrine and procedures, where applicable and consistent with US law, regulations, and doctrine.

For the Chairman of the Joint Chiefs of Staff:

DAVID L. GOLDFEIN, Lt Gen, USAF
Director, Joint Staff

Intentionally Blank

SUMMARY OF CHANGES
REVISION OF JOINT PUBLICATION 3-11
DATED 26 AUGUST 2008

- Numerous definitions added, revised, or deleted.

- Reorganizes chapter layout using the planning, preparation, execution, and assessment arrangement.

- Introduces hazard awareness and hazard understanding.

- Introduces and defines four new levels of chemical, biological, radiological, and nuclear (CBRN) hazard identification.

- Introduces contamination mitigation.

- Adds a contamination mitigation considerations appendix.

- Informed by the 2013 National Defense Strategy for Countering Weapons of Mass Destruction.

- Replaces the four S construct of sense, shield, sustain, and shape with prepare, prevent, protect, respond, and recover.

- Provides more discussion on mission-oriented protective posture.

- Adds discussion on military chemical compounds other than chemical warfare agents.

- Expands the discussion on the CBRN environment.

- Expands discussion on personnel decontamination.

- Adds an appendix on technical CBRN forces.

Intentionally Blank

TABLE OF CONTENTS

EXECUTIVE SUMMARY
COMMANDER'S OVERVIEW

- **Presents the Fundamentals of Operations in Chemical, Biological, Radiological, and Nuclear (CBRN) Environments**

- **Describes Planning and Preparation for Operations in CBRN Environments**

- **Addresses Execution of Operations in CBRN Environments, Including Protection Measures and Contamination Mitigation**

- **Explains Assessment of Operations in CBRN Environments**

Fundamentals

This publication focuses on maintaining the joint force's ability to conduct the range of military operations in a chemical, biological, radiological, and nuclear environment.

The threatened or actual employment of chemical, biological, radiological, and nuclear (CBRN) material, including toxic industrial materials (TIMs), can seriously challenge US military operations. The deadly, destructive, and disruptive effects of these weapons and materials merit continuous consideration by the joint force commander (JFC) and supporting commanders.

Strategic Context

The worldwide availability of advanced military and commercial technologies and information (including dual-use and emerging nontraditional threats), combined with commonly available transportation and delivery means, may allow adversaries opportunities to acquire, develop, and employ CBRN weapons without regard for national or regional boundaries. The Department of Defense (DOD) has expanded CBRN defense capabilities to address the complexities of the strategic context in which US forces may perform missions in CBRN environments.

Operational Context

The geographic combatant commanders (GCCs) support United States Government efforts, led by the Department of State, for countering weapons of mass destruction (CWMD) through interagency coordination, and security cooperation activities that help build certain capacities of other nations. Operating in a CBRN environment potentially impacts the freedom of movement and the preservation of combat power. Because of the potentially devastating consequences of CBRN hazards from intentional or unintentional release, measures are planned, prepared, executed, and assessed in order to enable forces to continue effective operations in a CBRN environment, as well as protect and mitigate the effects of CBRN hazards on military and nonmilitary personnel, equipment, and infrastructure.

Relation to the Joint Functions

Joint functions refer to related capabilities and activities organized into six groups: command and control, intelligence, fires, movement and maneuver, protection, and sustainment to help JFCs synchronize, integrate, and direct joint operations. Each of these joint functions may be affected by adversaries with CBRN weapons or CBRN hazards that develop into CBRN environments in the course of the execution of the primary mission.

Planning and Preparation

US forces should be prepared to conduct prompt, sustained, and decisive military operations in CBRN environments.

An adversary's use of CBRN weapons or TIMs released in the operational area can create effects that disrupt or delay operations to achieve US and multinational objectives. GCC planning normally takes into account potential adversarial CBRN weapons whether developing theater campaign plans or contingency plans.

Understanding the Chemical, Biological, Radiological, and Nuclear Operational Environment

Command staffs strive to provide a perspective of the interrelated variables that make up their specific operational environment (OE). joint intelligence preparation of the operational environment (JIPOE) should include a detailed analysis of the various CBRN threats and hazards. JIPOE analysts help the planning of efforts to mitigate the CBRN threats and hazards by evaluating the adversary's potential proliferation or employment of weapons of mass destruction (WMD), characterizing the effects of a WMD-related activity, and supporting the JFC's CWMD effort. The potential for accidental or deliberate release of CBRN elements within the operational area is also a major JIPOE analytic concern.

Strategic and Operational Planning

At the **strategic level**, the OE is analyzed in terms of geographic regions, nations, strategic personality of leadership, and political climate. Other factors that impact the combatant command's CBRN planning include treaties; international laws, customs, and practices; DOD policies; existing agreements/arrangements with host nations (HNs) en route to and within the operational area; and the capability of adversary propaganda to influence US public and world opinion. At the **operational level**, with regard to adversaries with CBRN weapons and US CBRN defenses,

JIPOE would concentrate on threats, friendly capabilities, and friendly vulnerabilities to CBRN threats and hazards.

Chemical, Biological, Radiological, and Nuclear Staff Assessment Components

CBRN threat assessment helps commanders make better-informed decisions about which protective measures to adopt. It helps identify the most likely CBRN threats and hazards that units and personnel will face, allowing units to identify the protective and vulnerability reduction measures most likely to keep them safe. Commanders conduct the friendly force capability assessment continuously from initial planning through all phases of the operation in determining how to employ forces and equipment in a CBRN environment.

Planning Considerations

The CBRN operational fundamentals of prepare, protect, prevent, respond, and recover apply across all operational planning phases (phase 0 through phase V).

The use or the threatened use of CBRN weapons can dramatically influence strategic and operational objectives and courses of action. Planners and commanders at all levels will integrate CWMD and CBRN defense and other force protection considerations into the overall planning and decision-making processes. During any phase of operations the combatant commander may need to support chemical, biological, radiological, and nuclear consequence management (CBRN CM) tasks including assisting HN forces as they conduct CBRN CM operations. If the OE contains CBRN weapons or storage facilities, then planning may need to include WMD elimination operations. In considering the challenges to sustained operations, eight areas merit special emphasis: intelligence support including conducting JIPOE; deterring adversary employment or proliferation; reducing vulnerability to adversary CBRN capabilities; preventing adversary CBRN weapon employment; performing force protection; conducting multinational operations; synchronizing operations; and assessing and managing risk.

Preparation Considerations

During preparation, the focus is on deterring and preventing adversaries from taking actions that affect combat power. The implementation of hazard awareness and understanding activities, protection of critical assets, and contamination mitigation measures with ongoing preparation activities assists in the prevention of negative effects.

Sustainment Considerations

The ability to sustain military combat operations with appropriate levels of logistics and personnel services is essential to operational success. Key considerations include the application of the joint logistic principles of sustainability, survivability, responsiveness, and flexibility to provide adequate CBRN-related equipment stocks and to support interoperability.

Execution

Joint operations require adaptability and flexibility during execution, particularly in CBRN environments.

During execution in a CBRN environment, the commander's staff identifies not only those key assessment indicators that suggest progress or setbacks in accomplishing tasks, creating effects, and achieving objectives for the overall mission, but also assesses how CBRN threats, hazards, and incidents have affected operations. JFCs should allow Service component and special operations forces, organizations, and capabilities to function generally as they were designed, including in CBRN environments. However, the JFC should account for differences in Service or component capabilities in CBRN environments when synchronizing operations.

Hazard Awareness and Understanding and Situational Awareness

CBRN hazard understanding is the dynamic individual and collective comprehension of the implications of CBRN incidents and resulting conditions within the OE, facilitating the framing of CBRN problems and decision making. CBRN hazard awareness is achieved through the fusion of CBRN detector information and collected intelligence data. The intelligence community collects and analyzes information about adversary CBRN capabilities and intentions along with other potential sources of CBRN hazards. CBRN hazard awareness leads to providing effective warning and reporting of threats to the force. Applying decisions based on the shared understanding of the CBRN situation also requires understanding when to deploy and employ CBRN defensive capabilities such as mission-oriented protective posture (MOPP) and collective protection (COLPRO).

Protection

Protection includes measures that conserve the force by identifying CBRN threats and hazards and preventing or mitigating the effects of CBRN environments.

CBRN-related protection includes measures that are taken to keep CBRN environments from having an adverse effect on personnel, equipment, or critical assets and facilities. Commanders implement protective measures appropriate to all anticipated threats, including terrorist threats and the use of WMD/CBRN or other sources of CBRN hazards. CBRN defense typically requires WMD active defense and CBRN passive defense and requires the planning, preparation, training, and execution of physical defenses to negate the effects of CBRN elements on personnel and materiel.

MOPP gear for individuals and COLPRO systems provide protection in CBRN environments.

WMD active defense includes measures to defeat an attack with WMD by employing actions to divert, neutralize, or destroy those weapons or their means of delivery while en route to their target. These are military-led activities (e.g., missile defense, air defense, and physical security) undertaken to defend against conventionally and asymmetrically delivered WMD.

CBRN passive defense includes measures taken to minimize or negate the vulnerability to and effects of CBRN incidents. Protection is a principle of CBRN passive defense, which focuses on maintaining the joint force's ability to continue military operations in a CBRN environment.

Emergency Management and CBRN Response Measures. Joint installation commanders manage and maintain comprehensive, all-hazards installation emergency management programs on DOD installations worldwide. DOD maintains this capability for its installations and, as directed, supports and assists civil authorities in emergency management activities for mitigating, preventing, protecting, responding to, and recovering from natural or man-made CBRN incidents.

Contamination Mitigation

The joint force applies contamination mitigation capabilities to maintain essential functions that must continue despite effects of hazardous contamination, or to enable the quick restoration of essential capabilities or combat power required to accomplish the current mission and achieve operational objectives. Contamination mitigation includes planning, initiating, and continuing operations despite the potential for CBRN hazards through the conduct of contamination control.

Sustainment Actions

Operations in CBRN environments make sustainment planning more complex.

Generally, operations will slow as tasks are performed by personnel encumbered by protective equipment or exposed to CBRN environments which may require abandonment or only limited use of contaminated areas, transfer of missions to uncontaminated forces, or avoidance of contaminated terrain and routes. Additionally, use of WMD or other CBRN incidents resulting in a major disruption of normal personnel and materiel replacement processes in the theater could severely hamper the commanders' capabilities for force generation and sustainment. Split-MOPP options could make available many forces that would otherwise have been unavailable due to unnecessary protective level constraints.

Assessment

Assessment of operations conducted in CBRN environments will increase the quantity and nature of variables that must be considered and analyzed to provide commanders with the most viable courses of action.

The staff should monitor and evaluate the following aspects of the CBRN environment as part of the assessment process:

- Changes to CBRN threats and hazards.
- Changes in CBRN force vulnerabilities.
- Changes to unit capabilities.
- Validity of assumptions as they pertain to CBRN defense.
- Staff and commander estimates.
- CBRN environments and their conditions and changes.
- CBRN resource allocations.
- Increased risks.
- Supporting efforts.

CONCLUSION

This publication provides doctrine for planning, conducting, and assessing military operations in CBRN environments.

CHAPTER I
FUNDAMENTALS

1. General

a. Hostile state and non-state actors, including terrorists and their supporters, who possess or are seeking to acquire weapons of mass destruction (WMD) materials, may pose a threat to the US and its allies. The threatened or actual employment of chemical, biological, radiological, and nuclear (CBRN) material, including toxic industrial materials (TIMs), can seriously challenge US military operations. The deadly, destructive, and disruptive effects of these weapons and materials merit continuous consideration by the joint force commander (JFC) and supporting commanders. The US military must train for and remain prepared to conduct the range of military operations throughout the operational environment (OE).

b. CBRN environments include CBRN threats and hazards and their potential effects. Operations in a CBRN environment will require the employment of strategic and operational capabilities and will require policies and procedures that will minimize or negate CBRN threats and hazards within an OE. This publication is applicable to joint force operations in a CBRN environment. Operations that occur in the US are unique and can have different laws, authorities, doctrine, and partners than operations conducted in a CBRN environment outside the US. For operations in a CBRN environment in the homeland, see Joint Publication (JP) 3-28, *Defense Support of Civil Authorities*, JP 3-27, *Homeland Defense*, and JP 3-41, *Chemical, Biological, Radiological, and Nuclear Consequence Management.*

(1) CBRN threats include the intent and capability to employ weapons or improvised devices to produce CBRN hazards.

(2) CBRN hazards include CBRN material created from accidental or deliberate releases, TIMs, chemical and biological agents, biological pathogens, radioactive material, and those hazards resulting from the employment of WMD, or encountered by the Armed Forces of the US during the execution of military operations.

(3) A CBRN incident is any occurrence involving the emergence of CBRN hazards resulting from the use of CBRN weapons or devices, the emergence of secondary hazards due to counterforce targeting, or the release of TIMs into the environment.

c. CBRN defense refers to the employment of tactical capabilities that counter the entire range of CBRN threats and hazards.

d. This publication focuses on maintaining the joint force's ability to conduct the range of military operations in a CBRN environment. It describes the environment in a strategic context while providing the necessary operational considerations, and describes activities and tasks that are conducted in joint operations. It is informed by the *National Defense Strategy for Countering Weapons of Mass Destruction* and works in concert with JP 3-40, *Countering Weapons of Mass Destruction*, and JP 3-41, *Chemical, Biological, Radiological, and Nuclear Consequence Management.*

e. This publication provides guidance to JFCs to assist in planning and conducting military operations in a CBRN environment. Whether resulting from deliberate or accidental release of CBRN elements, there are three types of hazards: chemical, biological, and radiological.

(1) Chemical hazards include any chemical manufactured, used, transported, or stored which can cause death or other harm through toxic properties of those materials. This includes chemical agents and chemical weapons (prohibited under the Chemical Weapons Convention [CWC]), as well as toxic industrial chemicals [TICs]).

(2) Biological hazards include any organism, or substance derived from an organism, that poses a threat to human or animal health. This can include medical waste, samples of a microorganism, virus, or toxin (from a biological source) that can impact human health.

(3) Radiological hazards include any nuclear radiation (i.e., electromagnetic or particulate radiation) that is capable of producing ions that cause damage, injury, or destruction.

For further information on operations in a CBRN environment, see Field Manual (FM) 3-11/Marine Corps Warfighting Publication (MCWP) 3-37.1/Navy Warfare Publication (NWP) 3-11/Air Force Tactics, Techniques, and Procedures (AFTTP) 3-2.42, Multi-Service Doctrine for Chemical, Biological, Radiological, and Nuclear Operations.

2. National Strategy

a. The *National Security Strategy* (NSS) identifies the need to reverse the proliferation of nuclear, biological, and chemical weapons and secure nuclear materials, as well as strengthen international peace and security. Success depends upon broad consensus and concerted action, moving forward strategically on a number of fronts by our example, our partnerships, and a reinvigorated international effort by countering those elements working to acquire WMD materials, as well as the goal of securing all vulnerable nuclear materials from terrorist groups. The NSS also addresses the need to engage with domestic and international partners to protect against biological agents and reduce risk. The NSS highlights nonproliferation concerns and examination of the *Treaty on the Non-Proliferation of Nuclear Weapons* (more commonly known as the *Nuclear Nonproliferation Treaty*) and special emphasis on stemming the spread of materials necessary to develop WMD.

b. Where proliferation or indigenous CBRN development has occurred, the principle US national objective is to deter an adversary's employment of CBRN weapons. To support deterrence, US forces should be prepared to operate effectively in CBRN environments. US forces need to mitigate the effects of CBRN weapon employment to fight and win in a contaminated OE. Operational success is dependent upon the joint force's ability to neutralize the adversary's CBRN capabilities. Success in these activities depends on accurate and complete CBRN risk assessments and mitigations, to include assessments that address adversary capabilities that may be used against US forces domestically or globally. Security cooperation activities can help shape the OE to dissuade or deter CBRN use. If deterrence fails, US forces may be called upon to conduct operations to neutralize CBRN threats.

See JP 3-40, Countering Weapons of Mass Destruction, *for more information on the various strategic measures available to the US to neutralize an adversary's ability to employ WMD.*

See JP 3-41, Chemical, Biological, Radiological, and Nuclear Consequence Management, *for more information on the US military response to reduce the effects of a CBRN incident.*

For chemical, biological, radiological, nuclear, and high-yield explosives (CBRNE)-specific guidance and standards for Department of Defense (DOD) installations worldwide to use when preventing, protecting against, mitigating, responding to, and recovering from CBRNE incidents, see Department of Defense Instruction (DODI) 3020.52, DOD Installation Chemical, Biological, Radiological, Nuclear, and High-Yield Explosive (CBRNE) Preparedness Standards.

3. Strategic Context

a. A variety of crises and conflicts challenge US interests. They include disputes and hostilities within nation states (e.g., insurgencies), and between and among nation states, coalitions of nation states, and transnational terrorists. These situations may threaten regional and global stability; and may involve the territory and populations of the US, its allies, multinational partners, other friendly countries, and a range of other US interests.

b. The worldwide availability of advanced military and commercial technologies and information (including dual-use and emerging nontraditional threats), combined with commonly available transportation and delivery means, may allow adversaries opportunities to acquire, develop, and employ CBRN weapons without regard for national or regional boundaries. Such situations could also expose US military operations to CBRN threats and hazards.

c. When their core interest or power bases are threatened, nation states may choose to disregard international protocols, agreements, and treaties. In some cases, nation states may be willing to acquire CBRN weapons despite being signatories or parties to international agreements and treaties forbidding such actions. Transnational terrorists do not consider themselves bound by such agreements and treaties. A continuously evolving asymmetric threat presents a variety of operational options for disrupting US forces by threatening attack using offensive CBRN capabilities. In an effort to circumvent defensive capabilities, several adversaries have the potential to use the expanding knowledge of chemical warfare and biological warfare (BW) or the global proliferation of relatively low-cost high technologies to develop new CBRN capabilities. US and friendly forces could be exposed to CBRN threats and hazards anywhere in the operational area and at any phase of conflict, even during peacekeeping or stability and support operations. Friendly force exposure to CBRN hazards could occur from an attack with militarized CBRN weapons or from releases of CBRN elements due to accident or from attacks on infrastructure, including urbanized industrial areas. DOD has expanded CBRN defense capabilities to address the complexities of the strategic context in which US forces may perform missions in CBRN environments.

4. Operational Context

a. The geographic combatant commanders (GCCs) support United States Government (USG) efforts, led by the Department of State (DOS), for countering weapons of mass destruction (CWMD) through interagency coordination, and security cooperation activities that help build certain capacities of other nations. However, building other nations' capacity for some aspect of CWMD is not necessarily a capacity for friendly forces to operate in a CBRN environment. With the exception of a number of allies, many of whom are charter members of the North Atlantic Treaty Organization (NATO), most of the host nations (HNs) where US forces are typically employed have primitive if any capabilities for operations in a CBRN environment. While the adversaries in those operational areas may not have CBRN weapons (i.e., known CBRN threats), other forms of CBRN hazards may be present that could result in CBRN environments. US forces must be capable of operating in those environments to accomplish the assigned mission that may not include any aspect of CWMD.

b. Even if an adversary does not intend to use a CBRN weapon, the existence of CBRN threats and hazards in any operational area creates potential risks. In addition to optimal intelligence of the CBRN threats, the existence of CBRN hazards in the form of TIMs must also be considered in each OE. CBRN hazards may be used for area denial and anti-access activities against US installations and facilities, ports of embarkation and debarkation, and the lines of communication between the US and its forces deployed to an HN.

c. **Military Support to Emergency Preparedness (EP).** EP consists of active measures taken prior to an incident to reduce the loss of life and property and to protect a nation's institutions from all types of hazards. JFCs support EP in a CBRN environment through development of a response plan, participation in joint and multinational exercises, and training of HN personnel and units on CBRN tasks. When suitable, CBRN forces are partnered with like HN capabilities to maximize the value of their specific expertise, to familiarize all forces with the capabilities and strengths of their counterparts, and assist in preparing for an incident. CBRN forces provide enduring or contingency support to a JFC for EP.

d. Clearly established supporting and supported command relationships provide clarity of military authorities and facilitate the effective interface with the interagency community. These clearly established relationships are required to reduce vulnerability and minimize the effects of CBRN threats employed against key HN installations, US installations and facilities, ports of embarkation and debarkation, and the US and its military forces and international allies.

e. Operating in a CBRN environment potentially impacts the freedom of movement and the preservation of combat power. Because of the potentially devastating consequences of CBRN hazards from intentional or unintentional release, measures are planned, prepared, executed, and assessed in order to enable forces to continue effective operations in a CBRN environment, as well as protect and mitigate the effects of CBRN hazards on military and nonmilitary personnel, equipment, and infrastructure.

5. Relation to the Joint Functions

Joint functions refer to related capabilities and activities organized into six groups: command and control (C2), intelligence, fires, movement and maneuver, protection, and sustainment to help JFCs synchronize, integrate, and direct joint operations. Each of these joint functions may be affected by adversaries with CBRN weapons or CBRN hazards that develop into CBRN environments in the course of the execution of the primary mission.

a. **C2.** C2 encompasses the exercise of authority and direction by a commander over assigned and attached forces to accomplish the mission. It includes those tasks and systems associated with understanding friendly CBRN defense capabilities and information systems, managing relevant information, and directing and leading subordinates in CBRN environments. The joint force has CBRN staff organizations and units that can characterize the CBRN hazard, develop a clear understanding of the current and anticipated CBRN situations, collect and assimilate information from intelligence, health, and specific CBRN reconnaissance and surveillance sources in near real time. The CBRN staff assess and provide actual and potential effects that may be created by CBRN threats and hazards. They can help the JFC identify those critical CBRN-related objectives and an end state so that the JFC may visualize the sequence of events in a course of action (COA) that moves the force from its current state to the envisioned end state. Operations in these environments will demand the integration of CBRN warning and reporting systems with civil defense systems to provide real-time warning and specific directions for action.

For additional information on the C2 function, see JP 3-0, Joint Operations, *and Army Tactics, Techniques, and Procedures (ATTP) 3-11.36/Marine Corps Reference Publication (MCRP) 3-37B/Navy Tactics, Techniques, and Procedures (NTTP) 3-11.34/AFTTP 3-2.70,* Multi-Service Tactics, Techniques, and Procedures for Chemical, Biological, Radiological, and Nuclear Aspects of Command and Control.

b. **Intelligence.** The intelligence function provides integrated, evaluated, analyzed, and interpreted information concerning foreign nations, hostile or potentially hostile forces or elements, and areas of actual or potential operations. Through the joint intelligence preparation of the operational environment (JIPOE) process, the intelligence function identifies relevant information about the OE and provides all-source information, including actionable intelligence, about the adversary's military system, including the anticipated military situation at the beginning of the operation, enemy centers of gravity, limitations, vulnerabilities, intentions, potential and most likely COAs, and priority intelligence requirements (PIRs). The CBRN staff collaborates with the JFC's intelligence staff to establish CBRN intelligence requirements and support the targeting of adversary WMD and identification of other CBRN hazards. The intelligence requirements address friendly force requirements and the enemy ability to use CBRN weapons (to include environmental factors and potential effects). Through intelligence, significant details such as determination and evaluation of enemy intentions, capabilities, types of agents, cover and deception methods, and sensors, protective posture, line of sight influences on direct fire, and friendly vulnerabilities to enemy strengths are understood. Information collected using CBRN reconnaissance and surveillance assets assists in confirming or denying intelligence. In a domestic environment the collection, analysis, and dissemination of information regarding the incident is called incident area assessment (IAA). IAA is essential for shared situational awareness among federal (including DOD), state, and local responders and is the keystone to ensure a timely, coordinated, and effective CBRN response. Protection relies heavily on the intelligence function.

See JP 2-0, Joint Intelligence, *and JP 2-01.3,* Joint Intelligence Preparation of the Operational Environment, *for additional information on intelligence aspects within a CBRN environment.*

   c. **Fires.** Fires utilize available weapons and other systems to create a specific lethal or nonlethal effect on a target. The role of fires in targeting CBRN threats includes the consideration and employment of lethal and nonlethal means to minimize, if not prevent, potential negative effects (e.g., CBRN incidents or conflict escalation). When operations are required in a CBRN environment, the JFC, component commanders, and unit commanders should determine the fires and maneuvers necessary to counter WMD threats and avoid CBRN hazards that could affect timely achievement of the JFC's objectives. Effects of fires must be observable and measurable to support the battle damage assessment and operational assessment processes. Adversary CBRN threats and significant indigenous CBRN hazards need to be identified and considered during the JIPOE and targeting processes. Pertinent information collected by the units for each target is maintained in the target folder for use in a future response. Consideration of potential collateral damage from attack on a CBRN facility must be factored into planning. Detailed weather, terrain, and population information must be assimilated and collateral effects mitigated to the extent possible. Commanders and CBRN staffs use target folders to facilitate the development of plans and integration of offensive operations and defensive operations that include CBRN passive and defensive measures.

See JP 3-09, Joint Fire Support, *and JP 3-60,* Joint Targeting, *for additional information on fires and targeting.*

   d. **Movement and Maneuver.** This function encompasses the disposition of joint forces to conduct operations by securing positional advantages before or during combat operations and by exploiting tactical success to achieve operational and strategic objectives. Accomplishing movement and maneuver in a CBRN environment can be more difficult, and in some situations the JFC or unit commanders may direct movement and maneuver to avoid areas contaminated by CBRN elements. Preserving combat power from the effects of CBRN incidents is essential for commanders to seize, retain, and exploit the initiative. Maintaining movement control, keeping lines of communication open, managing reception and transshipment points, and obtaining HN support are critical to CBRN defense and continuing operations in a CBRN environment.

See JP 3-0, Joint Operations, *for additional information on movement and maneuver.*

   e. **Protection.** The joint protection function focuses on the preservation of effectiveness and survivability of mission-related military and nonmilitary personnel, facilities, information, and infrastructure against all threats. The purpose for implementing CBRN defense measures is to provide the best possible protection against CBRN threats and hazards, to improve survivability by avoiding contamination, to continue the mission, and to reestablish the readiness of forces.

(1) JFCs rely on strategic guidance and use all available means including those of interagency and multinational partners to identify and analyze CBRN threats and hazards; plan to prevent and protect against CBRN threats, hazards, and their effects; and properly react to the effects of CBRN incidents. The combination of CBRN active and CBRN passive defense measures should help reduce the effectiveness of CBRN weapons or effects of unintentional release. Success depends on the effective use of unit and personal protective equipment (PPE); CBRN defense training; and proven protective tactics, techniques, and procedures (TTP). If an adversary succeeds in launching a CBRN attack and CBRN active defense measures fail to defend against it, CBRN passive defense measures become critical. These passive defense measures are designed to mitigate the immediate effects of a CBRN incident and to generally protect forces who are conducting military missions in a CBRN environment. Therefore, it is imperative that all commanders consider the CBRN threats and hazards; and if necessary, integrate CBRN defense into their mission planning, preparation, execution, and assessments, regardless of the mission type.

(2) CBRN defense requires the enabling support of unified action for friendly forces to operate in a CBRN environment and recover from CBRN incidents. However, many multinational partners and HN forces maintain very little if any capabilities for CBRN defense, despite regional adversaries with some form of WMD, or local CBRN hazards due to significant quantities of TIMs. Providing CBRN defense (active and passive), timely warnings of CBRN hazards, and being prepared to react to a CBRN incident are key to preserving the joint force's fighting potential. Protection relies on intelligence and C2 for indications of CBRN threats and incidents, which may be a challenge in multinational operations due to information sharing and complex command and organizational relationships.

See JP 3-0, Joint Operations, *and Chapter III, "Execution," for additional information on protection and aspects within a CBRN environment.*

f. **Sustainment.** Sustainment is the provision of logistics and personnel services necessary to maintain and prolong operations through mission accomplishment and redeployment of the force. Sustainment provides the JFC with the means to enable freedom of action and endurance and the ability to extend operational reach. Sustainment planning during all phases of an operation to include predeployment and redeployment planning must include operations in a CBRN environment due to the challenges inherent in normal sustainment operations as well as sustaining CBRN defense resources. The ability of sustainment planners to assess the potential effects of CBRN hazards and environments on their mission is a critical factor in deciding priorities for CBRN defense and efficiently allocating and moving resources. Normal logistics operations are adversely affected when supplies and lines of communications become contaminated. The requirement for protective equipment and resources further burdens the supply system and use of logistics assets. The CBRN environment will have a significant impact on site selection for logistics bases and the need for transshipment points, and dramatically increase the use of water for human consumption and decontamination.

See JP 4-0, Joint Logistics, *and JP 4-02,* Health Services, *for additional information on sustainment aspects within a CBRN environment.*

CHAPTER II
PLANNING AND PREPARATION

1. General

a. US forces should be prepared to conduct prompt, sustained, and decisive military operations in CBRN environments. An adversary's use of CBRN weapons or TIMs released in the operational area can create effects that disrupt or delay operations to achieve US and multinational objectives. The planning, preparation, and sustainment considerations contained in this chapter will assist JFCs and subordinate and supporting commanders with planning and preparation for military operations in a CBRN environment.

b. GCC planning normally takes into account potential adversarial CBRN weapons whether developing theater campaign plans or contingency plans. In addition to mapping WMD and establishing target folders, any planning for plausible, intentional, or unintentional releases of TIMs is wise when their concentration could cause a CBRN environment detrimental to friendly forces movement and maneuver, especially in urban industrial areas. Campaign and supporting plans must include options for generating adequate and timely force capabilities in the event of early adversary CBRN employment in the supported area of responsibility (AOR) or other/supporting areas, to include the US. GCCs establish PIRs and indicators to allow pre-incident actions to prevent surprise employment of an adversary's CBRN weapons and for the GCC's routine nonproliferation and counterproliferation activities to prevent acquisition or minimize capabilities for adversaries to launch successful CBRN attacks, and enable planning and actions to mitigate the effects of a CBRN incident.

2. Understanding the Chemical, Biological, Radiological, and Nuclear Operational Environment

a. Command staffs strive to provide a perspective of the interrelated variables that make up their specific OE. The OE is a composite of the conditions, circumstances, and influences that affect the employment of capabilities and bear on the decisions of the commander. JIPOE is the analytical process used by joint intelligence organizations to produce intelligence estimates and other intelligence products in support of the JFC's decision-making process. It is a continuous process that includes defining the OE; describing its impact; evaluating the adversary and other relevant actors; and determining adversary and other relevant actor COAs. As such, JIPOE should include a detailed analysis of the various CBRN threats and hazards.

b. Commander estimates, staff estimates, and collaborative information sharing help commanders continue to refine and deepen their knowledge and shared understanding of the OE. Estimates may require a constant reexamination of the OE that adopts a broader perspective of the situation, problems, and local challenges within the operational area. In multi-Service doctrine, operational variables that commanders and staffs at all levels should consider using for estimating and analyzing OE information are political, military, economic, social, information, and infrastructure (PMESII). During mission analysis at the tactical level, commanders and staffs can draw most of the relevant information needed for mission analysis from the more comprehensive PMESII analysis of their OE, using the mission variables of mission, enemy, terrain and weather, troops, and support available-time available, and civil considerations.

c. Commanders and staffs must continuously analyze their OE, progress of operations, and relevant CBRN factors, comparing them to the commander's initial vision and intent. Understanding the operational variables, their interaction with each other, and how relationships among those variables change over time helps commanders and staffs realize how, for example, the effects of CBRN threats and hazards on one or more operational variables can affect their OE.

d. The actual or threatened development, proliferation, or employment of WMD by an adversary can affect friendly forces by causing them to prepare for or conduct CWMD activities, and for a specific operation, plan and prepare for CBRN defense to include WMD active defense, CBRN passive defense, and contamination mitigation; and if directed, chemical, biological, radiological, and nuclear consequence management (CBRN CM) operations. JIPOE analysts help the planning of efforts to mitigate the CBRN threats and hazards by evaluating the adversary's potential proliferation or employment of WMD, characterizing the effects of a WMD-related activity, and supporting the JFC's CWMD effort. The potential for accidental or deliberate release of CBRN elements within the operational area is also a major JIPOE analytic concern.

(1) **Define the OE.** With regard to CBRN threats and hazards, the analysis of the OE should encompass the following:

(a) All adversary countries or groups as well as potential adversaries known or suspected of possessing a WMD capability and their intent or commitment to using it.

(b) All current and potential locations of adversary and potential adversary WMD delivery systems (e.g., missiles, artillery, aircraft, mines, torpedoes, and forces).

(c) All known and suspected adversarial CBRN hazards, nuclear capabilities, and their storage and production facilities.

(d) Asymmetric CBRN threats that would likely include a covert means of delivery (i.e., not WMD with overt military means of delivery) and potential targets.

(e) Advanced capabilities or weapons or materials capabilities (e.g., nanotechnology, biotechnology, advanced genetics, space-based capabilities, and advances in computing that would allow more efficient access to information or production techniques).

(f) Proliferation of WMD material, capabilities, expertise, and sensitive technologies.

(g) Friendly and neutral nation states' CBRN threats and hazards and their storage and production facilities within the operational area.

(2) **Describe the Impact of the OE**

(a) Identify and evaluate the vulnerability of key friendly logistic facilities and infrastructure to CBRN attack.

(b) Identify all known and suspected CBRN hazards in the operational area.

(c) Identify critical weather and terrain information needed to determine the effects of weather on potential CBRN hazards, regardless of the manner of release. Analyze the seasonal or monthly normal variations in weather patterns that might affect the use of CBRN weapons and their potential CBRN environments.

(d) Analyze the land and maritime surface dimensions to identify potential target areas for CBRN attack, such as choke points, key terrain, and transportation nodes.

(e) Identify state and non-state actors of proliferation concern.

(f) Identify CBRN-related material, capabilities, expertise, and sensitive/dual-use technologies.

(3) **Evaluate the Adversary and Other Relevant Actors**

(a) Analyze adversary and other relevant actor capabilities and intent to proliferate and/or employ specific types of WMD. Determine the locations, volume, and condition of adversary CBRN materials and potential hazards.

(b) Identify the specific types and characteristics of all adversary and other relevant actor CBRN-related delivery systems, with special attention to minimum and maximum operational reach.

(c) Evaluate adversary and other relevant actor doctrine to determine if employment of CBRN weapons is terrain oriented, force oriented, or a combination of both.

(d) Analyze the level and proficiency of adversary and other relevant actor training and experience in use of CBRN weapons and protective measures.

(e) Evaluate the practicality and timeliness of an adversary's and other relevant actors' exploitation of a new or different technology to develop a CBRN capability and delivery means.

(4) **Determine Adversary and Other Relevant Actor COAs**

(a) Identify friendly assets that the adversary and other relevant actors are most likely to target for CBRN attack.

(b) Determine locations where the adversary and other relevant actor is most likely to deploy CBRN delivery systems. These locations should be within range of potentially targeted friendly assets, yet still consistent with the adversary's deployment doctrine.

(c) Evaluate those characteristics of the adversary's and other relevant actors' CBRN stockpile that may dictate or constrain CBRN weapons use. These may include factors such as the quantity and yield of nuclear weapons, the age and shelf life of stored chemical munitions, and the production and handling requirements for biological agents.

(d) Determine types and quantities of CBRN weapons likely to be employed by an adversary and other relevant actors.

For additional information on JIPOE, see JP 2-01.3, Joint Intelligence Preparation of the Operational Environment.

3. Strategic and Operational Planning

a. **Strategic-Level Planning.** Planning activities at the strategic level establish national and multinational military objectives, develop global campaign plans and theater campaign and contingency plans to achieve those objectives, sequence initiatives, define limits, assess risk for the use of military and other instruments of national power, and provide military forces, in addition to other capabilities that support current strategic plans.

(1) At the strategic level, the OE is analyzed in terms of geographic regions, nations, strategic personality of leadership, and political climate. Other factors that impact the combatant command's (CCMD's) CBRN planning include treaties; international laws, customs, and practices; DOD policies; existing agreements/arrangements with HNs en route to and within the operational area; and the capability of adversary propaganda to influence US public and world opinion.

(2) Political factors, sociocultural factors, and economic characteristics of the OE assume increased importance for deterrence at the strategic level. They may, in fact, be the dominant factors influencing adversary COAs involving WMD. At this level, the analysis of the adversary's strategic capabilities will concentrate on considerations such as psychology of political leadership, national will and morale, ability of the economy to sustain industrial and technological capabilities for warfare, possible willingness to obtain or use CBRN weapons, and possible intervention by third-party countries and non-state actors, all weighed against US deterrence strategy and capabilities for attribution.

b. **Operational-Level Planning.** Planning at this level incorporates operational art and operational design elements during the initial stages of the joint operation planning process (JOPP). The size, complexity, and location of the OE at this level depends on the joint operations area assigned to the supported JFC and the complexity of the operation (i.e., based on the location of the adversary's political and economic support structures, its military support units and force generation capabilities, potential third-nation or third-party involvement, logistics and economic infrastructure, political treaties, press coverage, and adversary propaganda. At the operational level, with regard to adversaries with CBRN weapons and US CBRN defenses, JIPOE would concentrate on threats, friendly capabilities, and friendly vulnerabilities to CBRN threats and hazards. The use of threat assessments, capability assessments, and vulnerability assessments provides the commander and staff with shared understanding of the effects that may be created by CBRN incidents within the OE.

For detailed information regarding JOPP and the application of operational design (and operational art), see JP 5-0, Joint Operation Planning.

c. When examining the adversary's order of battle, the analysis of the adversary should include their doctrine for C2, logistic support, release procedures for the use of CBRN weapons and means of delivery, special operations forces (SOF), and paramilitary forces. Planning, supported by the JIPOE process, examines the adversary's COAs in terms of operational objectives, large-scale movements, lines of communications, and the phasing of operations. Mission analysis is used to study the assigned tasks and identify other tasks necessary to accomplish the JFC's mission. Operating in a CBRN environment should be one aspect of the mission analysis and the products form the basis for operational planning by identifying, developing, and comparing friendly COAs that would include assessing the impact of a CBRN threat or potential for CBRN incidents and environments on each friendly COA. Planning also helps to establish:

(1) The characteristics and decision-making patterns (i.e., CBRN weapons release procedures) of the adversary's strategic leadership and field commanders.

(2) The adversary's strategy, intention, or strategic concept of operation for use of CBRN weapons, which should include the adversary's desired end state, perception of friendly vulnerabilities, and intentions regarding those vulnerabilities.

(3) The adversary's ability to integrate use of CBRN weapons into their offensive or defensive operations in their overall concept of operations.

(4) The composition, disposition, movement, strength, doctrine, tactics, training, and combat effectiveness of adversary forces with an offensive CBRN capability to include:

(a) Principal strategic and operational objectives and lines of operation.

(b) CBRN weapons strategic and operational sustainment capabilities.

(c) Ability to create effects using the information environment.

(d) Use or ability to access data from space systems to support their targeting process.

(e) CBRN weapons and weapons storage location vulnerabilities.

(f) Capability to conduct attacks against globally distributed friendly force critical support nodes.

(g) Ability to conceal or obscure initial deployment of or their responsibility regarding deployment of CBRN weapons.

(h) Relationship with possible allies and the ability to enlist their support.

(i) Capabilities for force protection (FP), and protection of the civilian population and infrastructure.

(j) Identity of adversary personnel through the use of biometric data.

4. Chemical, Biological, Radiological, and Nuclear Staff Assessment Components

a. Threat Assessment

(1) CBRN threat assessment helps commanders make better-informed decisions about which protective measures to adopt. It helps identify the most likely CBRN threats and hazards that units and personnel will face, allowing units to identify the protective and vulnerability reduction measures most likely to keep them safe. When deciding on protective and vulnerability reduction measures, commanders and staffs must address two competing goals:

(a) Effectiveness. Effectiveness is adopting appropriate protective measures that will protect forces from specific threats that are most likely to occur.

(b) Efficiency. Efficiency is avoiding the adoption of unnecessary protective measures that have significant "costs" (financial costs or diversion of staff time, effort, and focus).

(2) CBRN threat assessment is not a one-time event, but a process of continuous reevaluations of CBRN threats and hazards throughout planning and execution to ensure that units continue to have appropriate protective measures in place. Forces should:

(a) Conduct an initial CBRN threat assessment during planning, before operations begin, and recommend the appropriate protective measures.

(b) Update the CBRN threat assessment at regular intervals (to help avoid subconsciously becoming habituated to previously identified threats and hazards) and whenever threats or hazards change.

(c) Modify CBRN protective measures as appropriate.

(3) The CBRN threat status is a flexible system used to assign the threat a serial number that is determined by the most current enemy situation as depicted by the continuously updated JIPOE process. This system allows local commanders to increase the threat status as conditions change in their operational area. Threat status governs the initial deployment of CBRN assets (equipment, specialized units) and the positioning of those assets in the operational area. The probability of threat is defined below.

(a) Serial 1 (Zero Probability). Opposing force does not possess CBRN defense equipment, is not trained in CBRN defense or employment, and does not possess the capability to employ CBRN weapons. Further, the opposing force is not expected to gain access to such weapons; and if they were able to acquire these weapons, it is considered highly unlikely that the weapons would be employed against US forces.

(b) Serial 2 (Low Probability). The opposing force has an offensive CBRN capability and has received training in defense and employment techniques, but there is no indication of the use of CBRN weapons in the immediate future. An indication may be the dispersal or deployment of CBRN materials/devices or the stated objectives and intent of opposing forces.

(c) Serial 3 (Medium Probability). The opposing force is equipped and trained in CBRN defense and employment techniques. CBRN weapons and employment systems are readily available. CBRN weapons have been employed in other areas of the theater. The continued employment of CBRN weapons is considered probable in the immediate future. Indicators would be as follows:

1. CBRN weapons or their normal means of delivery are deployed.

2. Enemy troops wearing or carrying CBRN protective equipment.

3. CBRN reconnaissance elements observed with conventional reconnaissance units.

4. CBRN decontamination elements moved forward.

(d) Serial 4 (High Probability). The opposing force possesses CBRN materials and delivery systems. CBRN defense equipment is available and training status is considered at par or better than that of US forces. CBRN weapons have already been employed in the theater, and attack is considered imminent. Indicators are:

1. CBRN attack in progress, but not in the current operational area.

2. CBRN warnings/signals to enemy troops.

3. CBRN weapons within range of friendly forces.

4. Movement of surface-to-surface missiles to a launch site.

b. **Friendly Capability Assessment.** Commanders conduct the friendly force capability assessment continuously from initial planning through all phases of the operation in determining how to employ forces and equipment in a CBRN environment. The capability assessment is a comparison of current unit capabilities for protection and CBRN defense, to include the proficiency of individual CBRN staff officers, command posts, cells, and elements, with the proficiency and resources required to support the commander. It involves the continuous assessment of unit plans, organization, manpower, equipment, logistics, training, leadership, infrastructure, facilities, and readiness. The following list provides a representative sampling of various CBRN-related capabilities that require continuous assessment:

(1) CBRN forces.

(2) CBRN staffs.

(3) CBRN equipment.

(4) CBRN reconnaissance and surveillance.

(5) Collective protection (COLPRO).

(6) Contamination mitigation.

(7) Automated warning and reporting.

(8) Hazard prediction and modeling.

(9) Preventive medicine.

(10) Casualty management.

(11) Analytical capabilities—in theater and available by reachback.

(12) Capabilities of partner nations and organizations.

(13) Incident/hazard risks.

5. Planning Considerations

a. Planning supports the commanders' decision cycle, and focused planning on how to conduct operations in CBRN environments helps the JFC to:

(1) Establish cooperative policies, procedures, and networks for the joint force, HN, and with other friendly forces to operate in a CBRN environment.

(2) Recognize the most likely CBRN threats and hazards from updated enemy tactics, capabilities, intentions, and the environment.

(3) Conduct assessments (threat, vulnerability, previous-incident/past-use, impact, hazard prediction modeling).

(4) Provide recommendations for the critical asset list and defended asset list.

(5) Coordinate unit protection measures, especially mission-oriented protective posture (MOPP) gear, COLPRO equipment, and decontamination equipment and procedures.

(6) Determine CBRN defense training and readiness requirements.

(7) Establish recovery and mitigation actions to match the CBRN threat and hazards, and if directed, be prepared to conduct or support CBRN CM or foreign consequence management.

(8) Coordinate CBRN health surveillance activities.

(9) Coordinate and integrate the CBRN defense actions of other interagency and multinational partners and the HN into the plan.

(10) Provide commanders' guidance for forces and facilities to ensure that they are prepared to operate in CBRN environments.

b. **Planning Considerations.** Specific planning considerations may vary considerably for all phases of a joint operation/campaign and at the strategic, operational, and tactical levels due to differences in the responsibilities and authorities at those levels for the application of C2, complexity of assigned missions, available resources, and the size of the operational areas and areas of interest (AOIs). The use or the threatened use of CBRN weapons can dramatically influence strategic and operational objectives and COAs. Planners and commanders at all levels will integrate CWMD and CBRN defense and other FP considerations into the overall planning and decision-making processes.

c. **Operational Fundamentals and Phasing.** The CBRN operational fundamentals of prepare, protect, prevent, respond, and recover apply across all operational planning phases (phase 0 through phase V). For each operational phase, the combatant commander (CCDR) plans to operate in a CBRN environment, set conditions preventing the emergence of a CBRN environment, and execute plans to respond to CBRN environments. The CCDR establishes priorities for applying CBRN operational fundamentals to planning based on CBRN threats and hazards in the OE. Figure II-1 illustrates an example of CCDR prioritization of those CBRN operational fundamentals for pre-incident, during incident, and post-incident periods that can take place at any time throughout operational planning phases.

d. **Directed CBRN CM and WMD Elimination.** During any phase of operations the CCDR may need to support CBRN CM tasks including assisting HN forces as they conduct CBRN CM operations. If the OE contains CBRN weapons or storage facilities, then planning may need to include WMD elimination operations.

See JP 3-41, Chemical, Biological, Radiological, and Nuclear Consequence Management, for additional information on CBRN CM and ATTP 3-11.23/MCWP 3-37.7/NTTP 3-11.35/AFTTP 3-2.71, Multi-Service Tactics, Techniques, and Procedures for Weapons of Mass Destruction Elimination Operations, for additional information on WMD elimination.

e. **Operational Challenges.** In considering the challenges to sustained operations, eight areas merit special emphasis: intelligence support including conducting JIPOE; deterring adversary employment or proliferation; reducing vulnerability to adversary CBRN capabilities; preventing adversary CBRN weapon employment; performing FP; conducting multinational operations; synchronizing operations; and assessing and managing risk. Information-related capabilities (IRCs) may be applied across these areas and independently. Each of these eight areas is discussed in more detail below.

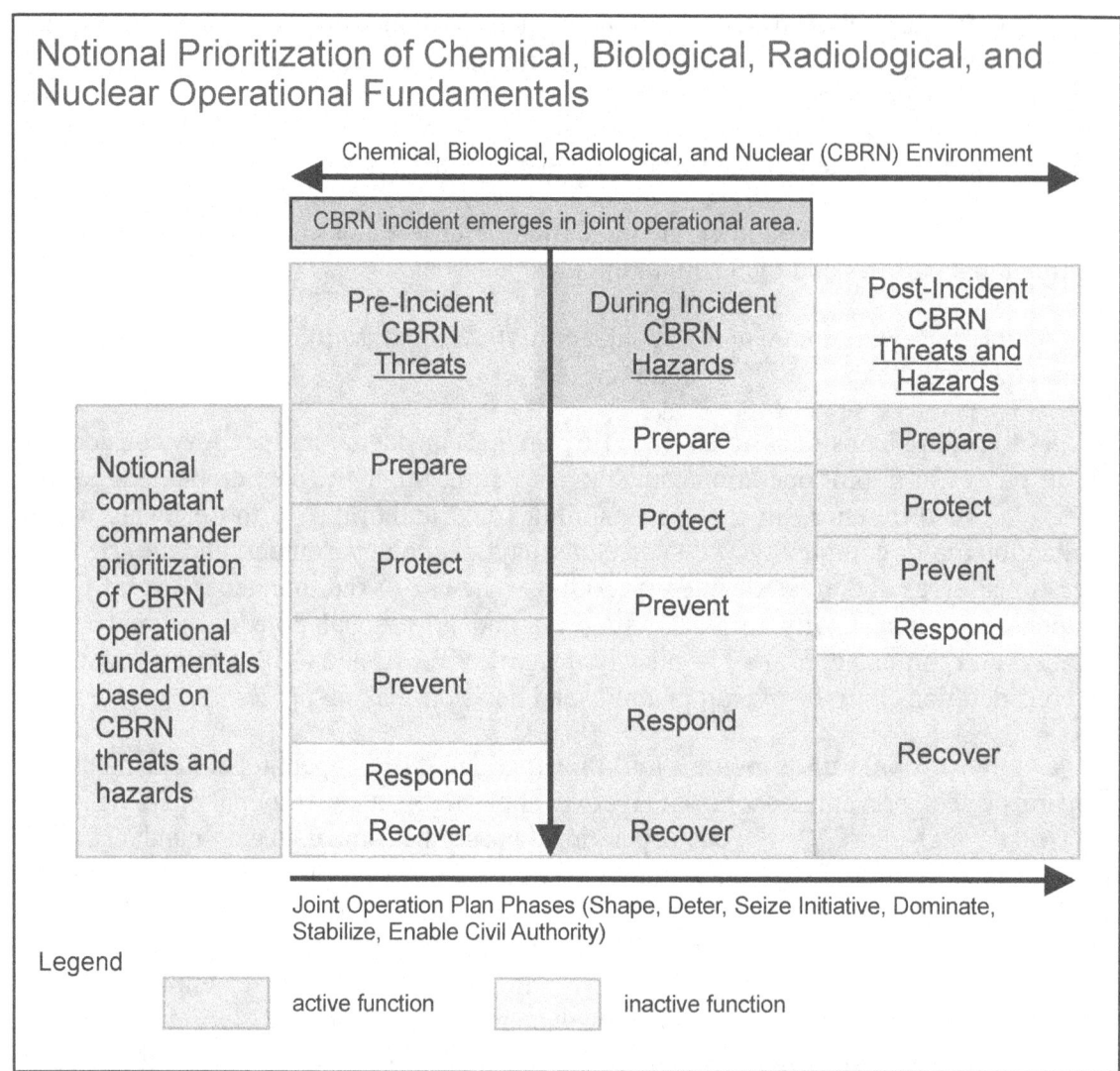

Figure II-1. Notional Prioritization of Chemical, Biological, Radiological, and Nuclear Operational Fundamentals

(1) **Intelligence Support.** The intelligence community and other joint staff members advise the CCDR and subordinate JFCs of an adversary's capability to employ CBRN weapons and under what conditions that adversary is most likely to do so. This advice results from integrated operations and intelligence planning, including red team utilization, during JIPOE, to ensure a continual assessment of the adversary's willingness and intent to employ these weapons. JIPOE includes defining the OE; describing the impact of the OE; evaluating the adversary; and determining adversary COAs. JIPOE should include an analysis of the capabilities and limitations of adversary CBRN weapons and delivery systems; their command, control, and release procedures; and the indicators of intent to employ CBRN weapons. Further, it should include information from the joint force surgeon, normally prepared as a part of medical intelligence, that identifies medical and disease threats in the operational area. Additionally, the JIPOE process should assess the potential for sabotage of industrial and commercial TIM sources that are vulnerable to intentional release by an adversary, or the unintentional release caused by an accident within

the operational area. JFCs, supporting, and subordinate commanders should include treaty, legal, and policy considerations relating to CBRN in their JIPOE process.

(a) JIPOE describes the process in which the adversary and other relevant aspects of the OE are analyzed to identify possible adversary COAs related to producing CBRN hazards and to support integrating CBRN threat considerations into joint operation planning, execution, and assessment. JIPOE analysts help mitigate the CBRN threat by assessing the adversary's potential proliferation or employment of CBRN weapons, characterizing the consequences of a CBRN-related incident, and supporting the joint force's CBRN defense effort. The potential for accidental or deliberate release of CBRN hazards within the operational area is also a major JIPOE analytic concern.

1. JIPOE analysis regarding adversary CBRN capabilities and intent is a particularly important prerequisite for military success during execution of a joint operation regardless of how the CBRN environment evolves. JIPOE provides the CCDR with an awareness of the evolving capabilities and limitations of adversary CBRN weapons and delivery systems, changes to their command, control, and release procedures, and the indicators of intent to employ CBRN weapons. The goal is to give the CCDR an understanding of the implications to the joint force of an actual or threatened CBRN contaminated environment to enable more effective decision making.

2. Both red teaming and wargaming are closely associated with joint planning (primarily in COA analysis). They are also used during execution to effectively assess decision points designed to deter or prevent CBRN weapon use, and to optimize joint operations in anticipation of the presence of CBRN hazards resulting from CBRN weapon use, industrial accidents, and sabotage.

(b) Intelligence, Surveillance, and Reconnaissance (ISR). ISR synchronizes and integrates the planning and operation of sensors; assets; and processing, exploitation, and dissemination systems in direct support of execution of current and future operations. As an integrated and operational function, ISR requirements must be specified and ISR missions executed in order to satisfy CBRN operational or technical threat requirements. ISR provides commanders and staff with the ability to understand adversary CBRN threat capabilities. Measurement and signature intelligence is conducted during both pre- and post-CBRN incident. Key to ISR visualization is an effective management process to graphically display current and future locations of ISR sensors along with CBRN reconnaissance and surveillance capabilities, their projected platform tracks, vulnerabilities to threat capabilities and meteorological and oceanographic phenomena, tasked collection targets, and products to provide a basis for dynamic redirection and time-sensitive decision making. This ability to redirect reconnaissance and surveillance capabilities allows the shift of planned or ongoing collection activities in response to changed or improved situational awareness or directive. The CCDR may also modify the commander's critical information requirements causing collection managers to reprioritize requirements.

See JP 2-0, Joint Intelligence, *for more information.*

1. Intelligence. Intelligence is exploited to obtain information about adversary CBRN capabilities, dispositions, intentions, and other potential sources of CBRN hazards (i.e., industrial facilities). The intelligence function is responsible for developing and tracking this information. When the intelligence concerns adversary CBRN capabilities, dispositions, and intentions, the CBRN defense community is also responsible for ensuring that CBRN technical requirements for information are satisfied.

2. Surveillance. The joint force will conduct sustained, systematic, and continuous observation of an area for unforeseen hazard releases and monitoring of known hazard locations. Surveillance facilitates situational awareness and maintenance of an accurate, high-fidelity, real-time picture of the OE as changes occur. Surveillance involves standoff or point (including those remotely dispersed, unmanned, and unattended) means to detect the presence or absence of hazards beyond the immediate vicinity of a friendly force to permit maneuver, avoidance of hazard locations, operations in stable environments, and support planning.

3. Reconnaissance. Reconnaissance provides the CCDR with data about activities or conditions in a particular AOI throughout the operational area. Effective reconnaissance enables the JFC to avoid contamination (e.g., affording safe passage) and preserve combat power by surveying an area or facility to provide detailed information on unforeseen hazards or monitoring an environment or facility for known hazards. Reconnaissance includes marking the hazardous area and supports sampling and hazard characterization capabilities.

For detailed information on tactical execution considerations, refer to Army Tactical Publication (ATP) 3-11.37/MCWP 3-37.4/NTTP 3-11.29/AFTTP 3-2.44, Multi-Service Tactics, Techniques, and Procedures for Chemical, Biological, Radiological, and Nuclear Reconnaissance and Surveillance.

(c) Medical Intelligence. Accurate and timely medical intelligence is a critical medical tool used to plan, execute, and sustain military operations. A supporting intelligence element should exist at some point in the medical unit's chain of command. This element, whether military or civilian, should be the primary source for the health services planner to access the necessary intelligence for the execution of health services operations. The health services personnel must develop a feedback system with the supporting intelligence element to provide and receive intelligence updates. Medical assets and information can save lives and maximize combat effectiveness by providing critical components of the installation and base passive defense, conducting tactical CBRN surveillance and identification missions, and by properly treating, stabilizing, and processing CBRN casualties. The deployed medical commander must be cognizant of operational intelligence pertaining to the CBRN threat. The deployed medical commander and key staff must have appropriate security clearances to access threat information. The medical commander along with key CBRN staff members should be integrated into the battle staff and CBRN cell, as tactically and situationally appropriate. Additional support may be provided by the National Center for Medical Intelligence.

(2) **Deterring Adversary Employment or Proliferation.** A fundamental premise of US military planning is that adversaries are most likely to be deterred from provocative action when US forces are sufficiently and visibly organized, trained, and equipped to defeat that action and fear a credible threat of undesired consequences. Deterring adversary use of CBRN weapons depends to a significant degree upon effective preparedness and operational readiness to deny the adversary any strategic advantage. Credible plans, education, and training, coupled with periodic exercises, and a clearly communicated commitment to hold an adversary and its leadership at risk in response to CBRN use are also important elements of deterrence. The adversary should perceive US capabilities and determination with certainty while remaining uncertain about the precise nature and timing of US countering actions. Synchronizing all IRCs provides the JFC, supporting, and subordinate commanders with the principle means to deter a potential or actual adversary from taking any CBRN provocative actions that threaten US national interests.

(3) **Reducing Vulnerability to Adversary CBRN Capabilities.** Vulnerabilities should be examined through continuous comprehensive assessments and integrated with risk management decisions that encompass the full range of potential targets subject to potential adversary CBRN attack. Commanders have multiple means to mitigate the consequences of identified risks and hazards in order to preserve combat power and minimize casualties. Such means include planning for branches and sequels in campaign plans, eliminating unique adversary network nodes, and assuring that multiple units are synchronizing operations to prevent CBRN attacks.

(a) When US, HN, or other civilian populations and infrastructures are at risk from a CBRN attack, the JFC assists the appropriate military and civil authorities in protecting, mitigating, and managing the consequences of these risks. Such efforts are often undertaken through a CCDR's building partner capacity program. Of particular concern to the JFC in this regard are CBRN risks to civilian areas that may affect execution of the military campaign.

(b) Assessments and resulting vulnerability reduction measures should also address the dangers posed by TIMs. Particular care should be taken in identifying the nature of such hazards, because in many cases, standard military CBRN individual protective equipment (IPE) may not provide the necessary protection. In some instances, avoiding the hazard may be the most effective or only COA. In all circumstances, the JFC should act to minimize immediate and long-term effects of toxic hazards, including low-level hazards, to health and mission objectives.

(c) CBRN vulnerability assessments are essential to FP planning. They provide the commander a tool to determine the potential vulnerability of an installation, unit, activity, port, ship, residence, facility, or other site against CBRN threats and hazards. The CBRN vulnerability assessment identifies functions or activities that are vulnerable to threats and require attention from C2 authorities to address improvement to withstand, mitigate, or deter against the threat. When improvements cannot be made, a risk-based approach to defense and protection activities must be undertaken.

$\underline{1.}$ The CBRN vulnerability assessment compiles the other types of assessments discussed into an overall snapshot of the unit's ability to support or conduct an operation given the specific OE and unit capabilities.

$\underline{2.}$ The CBRN vulnerability assessment will:

$\underline{a.}$ Identify vulnerabilities.

$\underline{b.}$ Determine the likelihood that CBRN threats or hazards will exploit a given vulnerability based on knowledge, technologies, resources, probability of detection, and payoff.

$\underline{c.}$ Predict the potential impact to the operational area if the vulnerability is exploited.

$\underline{3.}$ CBRN vulnerability assessments require a comparison of the threat with unit vulnerabilities to determine the efforts necessary to safely meet incident requirements. A vulnerability assessment also includes the integration of the commander's guidance through a risk management process to prioritize the implementation of vulnerability reduction measures.

$\underline{4.}$ Given the factors in the risk equation and the cost of implementing countermeasures, a determination may be made that the risk potential of a given vulnerability is not worth the cost of correcting or implementing a CBRN defensive countermeasure.

ATTP 3-11.36/MCRP 3-37.B/NTTP 3-11.34/Air Force Tactics, Techniques, and Procedures (Instruction) (AFTTP[I]) 3-2.70, Multi-Service Tactics, Techniques, and Procedures for Chemical, Biological, Radiological, and Nuclear Aspects of Command and Control, *discusses CBRN vulnerability assessments in more detail.*

(4) **Preventing Adversary CBRN Weapons Employment.** The JFC should not rely solely on efforts to reduce the force's vulnerability to CBRN attacks. CCDRs should make every effort to prevent the adversary from successfully acquiring and delivering CBRN weapons, using the full extent of actions allowed by the rules of engagement (ROE) and rules for the use of force (RUF). RUF apply to defense support of civil authorities operations in lieu of ROE. These actions could include WMD interdiction, close air support, strategic attack, WMD offensive operations, counterair operations, WMD elimination, collateral damage planning and assessments, early and sustained operations to disrupt or destroy CBRN capabilities, and establishment of multi-layered defenses against CBRN weapons delivery. Understanding the consequences of execution prediction and assessment for WMD targets and TIM sites is essential during the joint targeting process.

For more detailed information about preventing adversary CBRN weapons employment see JP 3-01, Countering Air and Missile Threats; *JP 3-03,* Joint Interdiction; *JP 3-40,* Countering Weapons of Mass Destruction; *JP 3-09.3,* Close Air Support; *JP 3-0,* Joint Operations, *and JP 3-60,* Joint Targeting.

(5) **Performing FP.** Fundamentally, protecting the force consists of those actions taken to prevent or mitigate hostile actions against personnel, resources, facilities, and critical information. These actions conserve the force's fighting potential. Offensive and defensive measures are coordinated and synchronized to enable the effective employment of the joint force while degrading opportunities for the adversary. FP is an integral part of managing the impact of force entry in anti-access and/or denied environments. CBRN protection must be provided throughout the entire operation: surveillance/reconnaissance through the actual assault and then resupply and refit. From the adversary's viewpoint, contaminating landing/drop zones and beach landing areas with CBRN hazards is a combat multiplier. Planning and considering a mix of types of protective resources helps balance operational requirements with optimal CBRN protection and sustainment.

(a) Force Health Protection. Medical protection of the force against CBRN threats involves integrated preventive, surveillance, and clinical programs. The JFCs and subordinate and supporting commanders' plans should include pre-exposure medical countermeasures (i.e., vaccination and prophylaxis), disease-containment strategies (i.e., isolation, quarantine, restriction of movement [ROM]), comprehensive health surveillance, CBRN contamination mitigation, diagnostics (including designation of field confirmatory and/or theater validation identification laboratories for medical specimens, and medical evacuation. These plans should take into account the capabilities and requirements of host countries, multinational partners, governmental and nongovernmental organizations (NGOs), and essential civilian workers supporting US and multinational forces.

(b) Protective Equipment. Sufficient equipment should be available to protect the uniformed force and mission-essential personnel. Individual and unit training for proper sizing, use, and care for IPE is required to take full advantage of its capabilities. IPE is the personal clothing and equipment provided to all military personnel to protect them from CBRN hazards. Protective equipment that meets civilian certifications as required by the US Department of Labor Occupational Safety and Health Administration is considered PPE. Protective equipment may include protective clothing and masks provided to shield or isolate personnel from hazardous materials.

(6) **Conducting Multinational Operations**

(a) US military operations are routinely conducted with forces of other countries within the structure of an alliance or coalition. An adversary may employ CBRN weapons against non-US forces, especially those with little or no defense against these weapons, in an effort to weaken, divide, or destroy the multinational effort. When conducting combat operations, the JFC should consider the capabilities and limitations of all available forces to maximize their contributions and minimize their vulnerabilities. Peacetime activities with multinational partners, particularly multinational and interagency training and planning exercises, provide means of preparing for multinational combat operations in CBRN environments.

(b) With very few exceptions, multinational operations will involve the use of HN sovereign airspace and territory, bases or civilian airports, facilities, and personnel (including non-USG and contracted civilian workers supporting US and multinational forces). For the CCDRs' theater campaign and contingency plans, HN considerations, including CBRN passive defense, are the subject of significant peacetime planning in which operational, legal, contractual, and personnel issues are addressed. Coordination of HN support activities will involve a number of interagency partners as well as the US country team. Particular emphasis is placed on early warning and detection; actions to prepare US and indigenous military forces; and protection of threatened civilian populations, essential infrastructures, and facilities. The GCC's staff should verify that all plans and exercises are in alignment with HN agreements for providing assistance to the HN during CBRN incidents, especially where effects may hinder US military response.

(c) Targeting chemical, biological, or nuclear facilities as a part of multinational operations may be constrained by differing treaty obligations, multinational ROE coordination requirements, and reporting requirements. The command staff judge advocate (SJA)/legal and arms control advisor should be involved in the planning and targeting processes to identify applicable treaty obligations, multinational ROE considerations, and reporting requirements.

For additional information on CBRN targeting, see JP 3-40, Countering Weapons of Mass Destruction.

(7) **Synchronization of Operations.** The objective of synchronizing operations is to maximize the combined effects of all friendly forces while degrading adversary capabilities. Synchronization entails the interrelated and time-phased execution of all aspects of operations, and is enhanced by situational awareness and adaptability. In CBRN environments, the requirements for successful synchronization include, but are not limited to, the proper integration of and sequencing among, for example, ISR capabilities, active and passive defense measures, offensive operations, CBRN CM, and sustainment. The JFC's operation or campaign plan, C2 arrangements, and TTP should facilitate synchronization across all force functions and components. Installation commanders must also synchronize base-level operations among all tenant units to maintain readiness and continuity of operations in CBRN environments.

(8) **Risk Assessment and Management.** Implementing all inclusive CBRN passive defense measures comes at a high cost. Providing full protection against CBRN hazards can significantly degrade the operational capabilities of the joint force. The JFC must balance the need to effectively implement CBRN passive defense against the cost and risk of these actions to his objectives and mission, and against the cost of having to recover force capabilities if passive measures are not enacted and an attack occurs. Use of risk assessment and management tools will enable him to effectively execute a risk mitigation strategy during operations in a CBRN environment.

f. CBRN planners and commanders must develop plans and implementation actions to counter potential adversary actions during peacetime and early in crises. These plans and activities require joint, multinational, and interagency coordination for activities that support CBRN awareness and understanding, protection of critical assets, and contamination mitigation measures.

(1) **CBRN Hazard Awareness and Understanding.** CBRN hazard awareness is the ability to exploit intelligence about CBRN threat dispositions and intentions and to determine the characteristics and parameters of CBRN hazards throughout the joint operating environment that bear on decision making and CBRN defense activities. CBRN hazard understanding is the ability to individually and collectively comprehend the implications of the character, nature, or subtleties of information about CBRN hazards and their impact on the operating environment, mission, and force, in order to enable situational understanding (see Figure II-2). Planning the collection and exploitation of the CBRN threats and hazards information is essential for the JFC's situational awareness. When CBRN hazard awareness and understanding is combined with an understanding of the enemy, it can be used to enhance decision making and planning requirements.

(a) Considerations for hazard awareness:

1. What CBRN threats may impact joint operations?

2. What are the adversary's cultural factors that might enable predictions about their motivation and COAs involving the use of CBRN weapons?

3. What industrial, medical, or research facilities may contain CBRN materials that could be used by an adversary to cause a CBRN incident?

4. What friendly operations may be the source of collateral CBRN hazards?

5. What are the types and locations of CBRN hazards present in the operational area?

6. What are the characteristics of the CBRN hazards?

7. In what concentrations or amounts are the hazards present?

8. How are the hazards being brought into the operational area if they don't already exist there?

9. What are the predicted generic and long-term effects of the CBRN hazards?

10. What are the environmental and climatology background data?

11. Identify naturally occurring diseases endemic to the local area and develop baseline medical and health surveillance data for those diseases.

12. What are the legal constraints to adversaries based on treaties and conventions?

Hazard Awareness and Understanding in the Joint Operational Environment

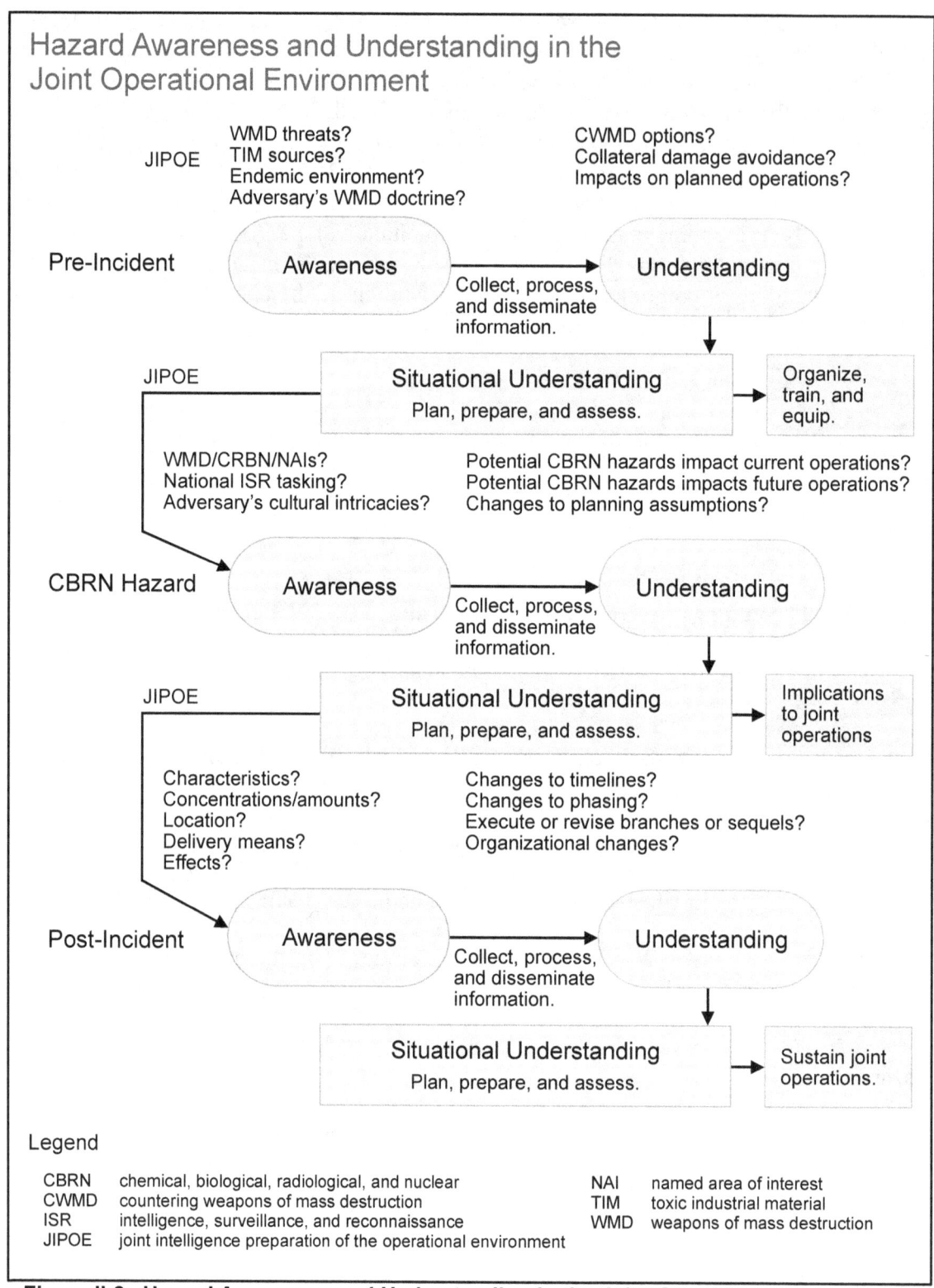

Figure II-2. Hazard Awareness and Understanding in the Joint Operational Environment

(b) Considerations for hazard understanding:

1. What effects do the potential sources of CBRN hazards have on current operations?

2. What effects will the potential sources of CBRN hazards have on future operations?

3. What are reasonable expectations for completing assigned missions in a CBRN environment?

4. Do any planning assumptions have to be changed?

5. What approaches need to be changed to facilitate the development of viable problem solutions?

6. What changes are there to the strategic environment?

7. What changes are there to the operational and tactical environment?

8. What timelines will need to be changed?

9. What phasing changes will be required?

10. What branches or sequels need to be executed or redone?

11. What organizational changes may need to be enacted?

12. What does the CBRN threat or CBRN hazard indicate about the adversary?

13. What are the JFC's current and future CBRN defense (active and passive) capability shortfalls and what can be done to mitigate these shortfalls?

14. What number of casualties is the hazard likely to produce?

(2) **Protection of Critical Assets.** Protection focuses on conserving the joint force's fighting potential in four primary ways: active defensive measures that protect the joint force, its information, its bases, necessary infrastructure, and lines of communications from an adversary's attack; passive defensive measures that make friendly forces, systems, and facilities difficult to locate, strike, and destroy; application of technology and procedures to reduce the risk of friendly fire; and emergency management and response to reduce the loss of personnel and capabilities due to enemy action, accidents, health threats, and natural disasters. Actions taken to protect the force include those that reduce the vulnerability of critical resources including personnel, facilities, and information to deter or neutralize incidents and their effects.

(a) Basic goals for operations and campaigns include prevention of adversarial use of CBRN weapons, rapid and uninterrupted force preparation and deployment, comprehensive FP, and adherence to the law of war.

(b) MOPP is not a fixed system and allows flexibility in providing maximum protection with the lowest risk possible, while still allowing mission accomplishment. Commanders may adjust the amount of MOPP gear required in their particular situations and still maintain combat effectiveness. Additionally, commanders can place all or part of their units in different MOPP levels (i.e., split-MOPP) or other variation within a given MOPP level.

(c) Separate MOPP systems exist for ship and land operations (see Figure II-3). JFCs should be familiar with both MOPP systems. Ship MOPP includes integrated detection, individual protection, COLPRO, and decontamination actions while land MOPP focuses on individual protection. In some circumstances, exposed ship or boat crews may be directed to use a land MOPP system in order to fully don protective equipment earlier in the process.

For more information on MOPP system flexibility, see FM 3-11.4/MCWP 3-37.2/NTTP 3-11.27/AFTTP(I) 3-2.46, Multi-Service Tactics, Techniques, and Procedures for Chemical, Biological, Radiological and Nuclear Protection, *and NTTP/Coast Guard TTP 3-20.31,* Surface Ship Survivability.

(d) Sustaining operations in CBRN environments may require COLPRO equipment, which provides a toxic-free area for conducting some activities and performing life support functions such as rest, relief, and medical treatment. In planning for the use of COLPRO, an assessment of the capabilities of the available COLPRO systems should be included. Proper planning and coordination with CBRN subject matter experts (SMEs) will assist in the effective use of COLPRO.

(e) When COLPRO is not available, plans must be developed, exercised, and evaluated to move personnel to alternative toxic-free areas that are well away from the contaminated areas. The use of split-MOPP procedures may be appropriate in such situations. If evacuation is not possible, building occupants may be able to shelter in place to gain limited protection by closing all windows and doors, turning off ventilation systems, and moving to closed, inner rooms. If there is advance warning, occupants can increase protection by sealing windows, doors, and openings, but must recognize that the building or space may quickly become uninhabitable without cooling or ventilation.

(3) **Contamination Mitigation.** Contamination mitigation is the planning and actions taken to prepare for and recover from contamination associated with all CBRN hazards to contain the spread of CBRN contamination and prevent the loss of assets. Planners must ensure that clear guidance for contamination mitigation is not confused with CBRN CM and is integrated into appropriate planning products. Staffs utilize CBRN hazard awareness and understanding (see Figure II-2) to match CBRN mitigation measures to the hazard, determine necessary capabilities needed to limit the spread of contamination and neutralize the effects, to prioritize and coordinate mitigation actions and resources, and

Joint Ship/Land Chemical, Biological, Radiological, and Nuclear Mission-Oriented Protective Posture Comparison

Ship MOPP		Land MOPP	
Ship MOPP Level	Description	Land MOPP Level	Description
MOPP 0	• IPE onboard and inventoried; all personnel sized and assigned IPE.	MOPP 0	• Carry mask; IPE available (within arm's reach).
MOPP 1	• IPE issued to all personnel and available (within arm's reach).	MOPP 1	• Don protective suit.
MOPP 2	• Carry mask, other IPE available. • Activate detectors. • Set condition MODIFIED ZEBRA.	MOPP 2	• Don protective boots.
MOPP 3	• Don protective suit. • Don protective boots. • Set condition ZEBRA (ship hatch closure/secure measures). • Activate intermittent washdown.	MOPP 3	• Don protective mask. • Secure hood.
MOPP 4	• Don protective mask. • Secure hood. • Don protective gloves. • Set condition CIRCLE WILLIAM (ship hatch closure/secure measures) as required. • Activate continuous washdown.	MOPP 4	• Don protective gloves.

Legend

IPE   individual protective equipment   MOPP   mission-oriented protective posture

Figure II-3. Joint Ship/Land Chemical, Biological, Radiological, and Nuclear Mission-Oriented Protective Posture Comparison

establish measures to assess mitigation efforts. A proactive approach to contamination mitigation is achieved through planning and preparation.

g. **Other Planning Considerations**

(1) **IRCs.** The integrated employment of IRCs may reduce force vulnerability and help deter adversarial use of CBRN weapons. Public interest in and fear of CBRN-related developments may be intense and may affect US and multinational leadership decisions. National-level communications can create international and internal pressures to convince an adversary not to acquire or use CBRN weapons. Fully explaining the USG position on the potential US reaction in the event of an adversary use of CBRN materials on US or multinational forces could be very beneficial. A combination of IRCs, including electronic warfare, cyberspace operations, military information support operations, military deception, and operations security to influence, disrupt, corrupt, or usurp the adversary's decision-making process can be vital to the success of the overall operation or campaign. To affect an adversary's intelligence collection and situational awareness, IRCs may help prevent an adversary from acquiring information necessary to successfully target friendly forces and facilities using CBRN weapons.

(2) **Public Affairs.** The JFC should provide, as the situation requires, timely and accurate information to the public, regarding actions taken in reaction to CBRN threats, hazards, or incidents. The JFC and the staff public affairs officer are the primary official military spokespersons for this purpose.

For further details on public affairs, see JP 3-61, Public Affairs.

(3) **Legal Guidance.** The complexity of CBRN and associated law and policy require continuous involvement of the SJA, or appropriate legal advisor with the planning, control, and assessment of operations. Because of the global nature of some CBRN threats, this will also include continuous consultation with interagency and multinational partners, HN governments, and intergovernmental organizations (IGOs) to establish the necessary legal authorities, capabilities, and limitations associated with their organizations. The SJA can advise the JFC and staff of potential associated legal issues (e.g., compliance with federal environmental laws and regulations; quarantine and isolation enforcement issues; and targeting in a CBRN environment).

(a) **International Law and Agreements.** The SJA will advise the JFC and staff on international law and international agreements that may impose certain legal obligations on the US and shape the planning of joint operations and campaigns associated with CBRN threats and environments (e.g., international agreements on status of forces, logistics support, and security assistance). These legal requirements may impose constraints and restraints. They will shape the planning of an operation or campaign associated with CBRN threats and hazards.

(b) **Arms Control and Nonproliferation Treaties.** Arms control and nonproliferation treaties establish global norms opposing the proliferation of WMD, their precursors, means of delivery, and weapons manufacturing equipment. Treaties provide international standards to be adhered to by signatories. International treaties provide diplomatic tools and legal recourse to isolate and punish violators.

6. Preparation Considerations

a. The force is most often vulnerable to surprise and attack during preparation. Preparation creates conditions that improve the friendly forces' opportunities for success and requires the commander to ensure that the force is trained, equipped, and ready to execute operations. Preparation activities help commanders and their staffs and forces to understand the operational situation and their roles. During preparation, the focus is on deterring and preventing adversaries from taking actions that affect combat power. The implementation of hazard awareness and understanding activities, protection of critical assets, and contamination mitigation measures with ongoing preparation activities assists in the prevention of negative effects.

b. The fundamental elements for maintaining adequate preparedness require a clear understanding of the threats and operational requirements, both overseas and in the US. To support these requirements, the commanders' mission analyses identify specific, mission-essential tasks for individuals and organizations that facilitate operations in CBRN environments. DOD also is responsible for homeland defense against employment of CBRN weapons directly against the US, and supporting homeland security against possible covert CBRN threats. Domestic military support is subject to constitutional, statutory, and policy restrictions.

c. Complete intelligence collection and analysis for each specific threat assessment is seldom available. Changes in the perceived magnitude or severity of the threat when compared to friendly vulnerability and risk limitations often dictate adjustments or changes to the plan when those threat characteristics exceed friendly force limitations established in planning. During preparation, the staff continues to monitor and evaluate the overall situation and update the commander's critical information requirements, because variable threat and hazard assessments may generate new PIRs, while significant changes in friendly assets' capabilities or vulnerabilities could lead to new friendly force information requirements.

d. Commanders and staffs consider the following during preparation:

(1) Revise and refine the plan.

(2) Employ systems to detect CBRN threats and hazards and provide early warning of any hostile activities.

(3) Collect and analyze CBRN threat and hazard data.

(4) Monitor both adversary and joint force preparation activities and revise assessments.

(5) Request support to reinforce logistical preparations and replenishment.

(6) Assess joint force Service components training and readiness requirements.

(7) Expedite the procurement and availability of resources needed for protection against CBRN weapons.

(8) Synchronize efforts with USG departments and agencies and multinational partners.

(9) Monitor forces and facilities to ensure preparation to operate in CBRN environments.

e. As the staff monitors and evaluates the performance or effectiveness of the friendly COAs, intelligence assets collect information that may verify adversary COAs. As the threat changes, risk to the force changes, so some changes may require a different CBRN protective posture or the implementation or cessation of specific CBRN measures and activities. The staff analyzes changes or variances that may require modifications to the priorities and obtains additional commander's guidance when necessary.

(1) Specific activities to enhance hazard awareness understanding during preparation may focus on the collection and exploitation of information gained from CBRN reconnaissance and surveillance as well as from medical surveillance to develop and refine the common operational picture of the OE. Relevant information collections can help fill in information gaps, refine potential threats and hazards data into facts, validate assumptions, and finalize the plan.

(2) Multiple sources provide units with relevant information, which is processed, extracted, formatted, and forwarded. Commanders and their staffs evaluate the information to assess its impact on operations and protection. The assessment may lead to directives/orders to help protect against the effects of the assessed CBRN hazard. Commanders may direct an integrated series of protective measures (e.g., adjust MOPP) to decrease the level of risk (e.g., decrease threat of exposure), and the plan is revised as updated information is received. MOPP analysis of the appropriate levels of protection based on hazards, mission, environmental conditions, and time constraints will inform the commander's decision.

(3) Forces prepare for contamination mitigation activities by monitoring current operations, assessing resource readiness, preparing mitigation packages (structures and resources to include medical), and synchronizing the contamination mitigation capabilities to ensure they are ready to respond. Some situations require unique application of decontamination principles, procedures, and methods. These considerations should take into account command, control, communications, and planning capabilities required for decontamination of strategically significant areas/terrain or facilities. Other factors requiring consideration include standing up/deactivating a task force, selecting and defining joint decontamination operations sites, and establishing the manning allocation of initial headquarters for such decontamination operations.

For additional decontamination considerations see Appendix E, "Contamination Mitigation Considerations."

For specific information on tactical decontamination operations and levels, see FM 3.11.5/MCWP 3-37.3/NTTP 3-11.26/AFTTP(I) 3-2.60, Multi-Service Tactics, Techniques, and Procedures for Chemical, Biological, Radiological, and Nuclear Decontamination.

(a) Patient decontamination reduces the threat of CBRN contamination to medical personnel, other patients, and the health care facility. Patient decontamination is accomplished as the operation and patient load allows. Treatment for stabilization to conduct patient decontamination should be delayed only if it does not put the patient at additional risk. Trained and qualified triage personnel determine priority of treatment and decontamination. Aeromedical evacuation capabilities for contaminated and contagious casualties are very limited. Consultation between the JFC and United States Transportation Command (USTRANSCOM) regarding the issue of evacuation or treatment in place is appropriate.

(b) Sensitive equipment decontamination considers the delicate nature of certain types of equipment (e.g., avionics and/or electrical, electronic, and environmental systems); aircraft and vehicle interiors; associated cargo; and some weapon systems. Due to the corrosive properties of most decontamination solutions, sensitive equipment decontamination options are limited. Best practices include employing contamination avoidance measures (to include COLPRO and standoff/point detection systems) to prevent or mitigate the effects to the interior contamination of vehicles, aircraft, and ships.

(c) Aircraft pose unique decontamination challenges. Spot decontamination can be used as an immediate measure to mitigate unintentional transfer and spread contamination on aircraft that may require servicing between sorties, to support ingress and egress of aircraft by crews and passengers, or if performing pre- or post-flight inspections; however, clearance decontamination is required for unrestricted use of aircraft for international flight operations, transportation, and maintenance. See Appendix E, "Contamination Mitigation Considerations," for additional information on aircraft decontamination considerations.

(d) Sealift Decontamination. Clearance decontamination may be required to ensure the unrestricted use of Military Sealift Command (MSC) ships for strategic sealift. To achieve this level of cleanliness, specialized teams with more sensitive detection equipment may be required. Considerations must include limited shipyard and contractor resource capabilities for conducting decontamination operations at the clearance level. Therefore, the JFC should strive to limit the intentional CBRN exposure of MSC strategic sealift ships to only those missions considered critical. JFC plans must take into account these challenges in considering employment of MSC ships to transport contaminated cargo or passengers or to operate in contaminated areas.

(e) Fixed site decontamination techniques focus on fixed facilities and mission support areas, such as communications systems, C2 facilities, intelligence facilities, supply depots, aerial and sea ports, medical facilities, and maintenance sites.

(f) Cargo Decontamination. Contaminated cargo must be packaged safely in accordance with hazardous materials procedures or decontaminated prior to transport. To limit the spread of contamination and minimize risks to personnel, the JFC will limit the retrograde of contaminated or formerly contaminated cargo to "critical" items that are preidentified in JFC plans unless the cargo has been assessed to be safe or meets clearance standards. Every effort will be made to provide shipment traceability of contaminated or formerly contaminated cargo. Additionally, destination and transit countries may deny overflight and landing clearances to aircraft carrying contaminated cargo. US Presidential approval may be required for these shipments. Post conflict redeployment of contaminated assets may require extensive decontamination measures (to include extended weathering) and the use of specialized teams and highly sensitive detection and monitoring equipment. In place destruction/disposal of contaminated equipment may be necessary; detailed documentation pertaining to the in place destruction of contaminated material will be retained by appropriate authorities.

(g) Terrain Decontamination. Absorption of CBRN hazards by terrain surfaces may result in delayed exposure. The decontamination of terrain allows personnel to increase stay time in an area and provides passage through an area. Large-scale terrain decontamination requires extensive resources in terms of equipment, material, and time; and must therefore be limited to areas of critical importance.

7. Sustainment Considerations

a. The ability to sustain military combat operations with appropriate levels of logistics and personnel services is essential to operational success. Plans supporting deployment, reception, staging, onward movement, and integration (RSOI), and sustainment must continually be reviewed and updated, as needed. This includes, but is not limited to:

(1) Coordinating the resupply of CBRN defense and monitoring equipment. Some CBRN-related equipment is often commercial-off-the-shelf items that may need special consideration for maintenance and replacement.

(2) Coordinating the supply of food, potable water, fuel, arms, munitions, and equipment.

(3) Providing for maintenance of equipment.

(4) Coordinating field services, personnel services, health services, mortuary affairs, religious affairs, legal services, financial management support, and medical readiness.

(5) Building and maintaining sustainment bases; assessing, repairing, and maintaining infrastructure.

(6) Providing common-user logistic support.

(7) Establishing and coordinating movement services.

(8) Maintaining force health protection measures.

(9) Contamination mitigation.

b. Maintaining adequate logistic support is more difficult for operations in CBRN environments. Key considerations include the application of the joint logistic principles of sustainability, survivability, responsiveness, and flexibility to provide adequate CBRN-related equipment stocks and to support interoperability. The application of these principles in a CBRN environment is described as follows:

(1) Sustainability. Sustainability is the measure of the ability to maintain logistic support to all users throughout the theater for the duration of the operation. In CBRN environments, constant, long-term consumption of CBRN defense supplies requires careful planning, monitoring serviceability for items, such as IPE that have specific shelf lives (i.e., expiration dates), and anticipation of future requirements. In an active CBRN environment, water usage will dramatically increase both for human consumption and decontamination.

(2) Survivability. Theater logistic sites and units present an adversary with important and often high-value fixed targets for attack with CBRN weapons. Protection planning must include both active and passive defense measures to minimize the risks from CBRN attacks while satisfying the needs of the joint force for uninterrupted logistic support.

(3) Responsiveness. The potential damage and environmental conditions caused by CBRN incidents may require relocation of bases and medical facilities, major redirection of supply flow, reallocation of transportation and engineering services, and short-notice transfer of replacement personnel or units from one part of the theater to another. Joint force plans should allow for surges in logistic requirements for CBRN defense consumables and equipment items to appropriate units.

(4) Flexibility. Work/rest cycles must be activated and implemented to the maximum practical extent allowed. Maintaining logistic flexibility in CBRN environments requires that logistic units be capable of rapid alteration of work schedules. CBRN incidents can cause degradation of logistic operations due to having to operate in protective clothing and handle and decontaminate supplies and equipment. Logistics plans need to include means for protective covering and sheltering of essential items against contamination.

(5) CBRN Defense Equipment Stocks. Logistic support for CBRN defense readiness includes providing adequate supplies and transportation of CBRN defense equipment, as well as assisting as necessary any CBRN defense organizations directly responsible for carrying out reconnaissance, decontamination, and supporting tasks.

(6) Interoperability. In operations outside the continental US, when the JFC will likely be working with HN and other forces, each member organization of a multinational operation is responsible for its own CBRN defense, but the ability to exploit logistic interoperability (e.g., in equipment and supplies) can contribute to the effectiveness of the collective CBRN defense.

(7) Training. Individual and unit survival skills and the ability to perform mission-oriented tasks while in protective clothing are vital to theater logistic activities. Mission-

essential tasks will be identified in theater plans and unit standard operating procedures, and regular training should be conducted to establish individual and unit proficiency.

c. Logistics Supportability Analysis. The logistics supportability analysis provides a broad assessment of core logistics capabilities required to execute plans and define the total logistics requirement for execution of a concept of operations. Because of the potential impact of CBRN contamination on logistics support and support requirements, collaboration with CBRN experts is essential in this process. The CBRN staff can highlight potential deficiencies in supply forecasts (protective equipment, decontaminants, and filters) that may result from contamination; risks to the logistics support mission attributed to CBRN threats; and additional CBRN defense capability requirements that may result from exposure of logistics units, equipment, or facilities to CBRN contamination.

d. Operating tempo (OPTEMPO), logistics, the health services, personnel services, and reconstitution efforts may be affected by the introduction of CBRN hazards and can present separate and distinct threats to personnel, units, equipment, and operations. The ability to assess the potential effects of CBRN weapons and hazards on the mission is a critical factor in deciding priorities for CBRN protection and efficiently allocating resources.

See Appendix E, "Contamination Mitigation Considerations," for additional decontamination considerations.

CHAPTER III
EXECUTION

1. General

a. Joint operations require adaptability and flexibility during execution, particularly in CBRN environments. The application of operational art and operational design provides the operational approach and promotes unified action for planning and execution.

b. Execution puts the joint operation planning described in Chapter II , "Planning and Preparation," into action to accomplish the mission. During execution, situational understanding acquired through CBRN hazard awareness and understanding is used to support decision making, especially for execution and planning adjustment decisions.

(1) During execution in a CBRN environment, the commander's staff identifies not only those key assessment indicators that suggest progress or setbacks in accomplishing tasks, creating effects, and achieving objectives for the overall mission, but also assesses how CBRN threats, hazards, and incidents have affected operations.

(2) Assessment recommendations help commanders adjust operations and the application of resources, determine when to develop and execute appropriate branches and sequels, and ensure current and future operations remain aligned with the mission and military end state (see Chapter IV, "Assessment," for additional information). Execution continues until the mission is accomplished and/or termination criteria have been met.

c. Along with unity of command, centralized planning and direction and decentralized execution are key considerations in how JFCs organize and employ their forces. While JFCs may elect to centralize some functions, they should avoid reducing the versatility, responsiveness, and initiative of subordinate forces. JFCs should allow Service component and SOF, organizations, and capabilities to function generally as they were designed, including in CBRN environments. However, the JFC should account for differences in Service or component capabilities in CBRN environments when synchronizing operations. Commanders should use situational leadership to maximize operational performance and overcome the ambiguities and uncertainties inherent in combat operations, especially when faced with a CBRN environment.

For detailed information on tactical execution considerations, refer to FM 3-11/MCWP 3-37./NWP 3-11/AFTTP 3-2.42, Multi-Service Doctrine for Chemical, Biological, Radiological, and Nuclear Operations*, and FM 3-05.132,* Army Special Operations Forces Chemical, Biological, Radiological, and Nuclear Operations*.*

2. Hazard Awareness and Understanding and Situational Awareness

a. The JFC and staff must have the ability to share information and create the shared understanding which is required to make informed and timely decisions amid massive quantities of operational data. Even a small or isolated CBRN incident may produce significant quantities of data that challenge decision makers if the capability to evolve from initial data gathering to full situational awareness does not exist. There is an evolution from a first bit of data provided by a CBRN sensor (or a group of sensors linked to provide a more complete picture of a large facility, city, or region) to full situational awareness of the implications of a CBRN incident based on shared information. The information concerning the causes of CBRN incidents and environments (hazard awareness) have to be properly processed, managed, and shared to create the necessary shared understanding (hazard understanding) that results in the wisdom essential to sound decision making.

For a more detailed discussion of creating a shared understanding, see JP 3-0, Joint Operations.

b. **CBRN Hazard Understanding.** CBRN hazard understanding is the dynamic individual and collective comprehension of the implications of CBRN incidents and resulting conditions within the OE, facilitating the framing of CBRN problems and decision making.

c. CBRN threat and hazard warnings and reporting play a role in awareness, primarily at the strategic and operational levels.

(1) Strategic-Level Warning. The joint global warning enterprise (JGWE) provides an inclusive, visible, and unified means to provide information to policy makers, planners, and operators to assist in shaping strategic outcomes. The JGWE supports CWMD issues by leveraging CBRN SMEs through regional strategic country communities of interest and as a panel member of the intelligence community's CBRN threat working group. Additionally, the JGWE provides CBRN strategic warning to address risk factors and counterproliferation issues.

(2) Operational-Level Warning. Awareness of a CBRN hazard results in warning, alerting, and reporting that provide hazard data which is key to decentralized operational decisions at all levels within the joint force. Awareness allows for the rapid warning and alerting of affected personnel who employ CBRN protective equipment and mitigation capabilities to negate the effects of the CBRN incident and help sustain operations. The JFC processes this awareness of a CBRN incident to gain an understanding of its implications to joint operations.

For more information on CBRN warning and reporting, refer to FM 3-11.3/MCRP 3-37.2A/NTTP 3-11.25/AFTTP(I) 3-2.56, Multi-Service Tactics, Techniques, and Procedures for Chemical, Biological, Radiological, and Nuclear Contamination Avoidance.

d. CBRN hazard awareness is achieved through the fusion of CBRN detector information and collected intelligence data. The intelligence community collects and analyzes information about adversary CBRN capabilities and intentions along with other potential sources of CBRN hazards. When intelligence concerns adversary CBRN capabilities, dispositions, and intentions, the CBRN defense community is responsible for ensuring that CBRN technical information requirements are satisfied. As part of the JIPOE process, neutral and friendly activities that may be sources of potential CBRN hazards also are considered and analyzed.

e. CBRN hazard awareness leads to providing effective warning and reporting of threats to the force. CBRN hazard awareness and understanding encompass the following questions:

(1) What CBRN threats may affect operations (current/future)?

(2) What are the adversary's sociocultural factors that might enable predictions of motivations and COAs for using CBRN weapons and devices?

(3) What friendly operations may be the source of collateral CBRN hazards?

(4) What industrial, medical, or research facilities may play a role in a CBRN (including TIM) incident occurring?

(5) Where are TIM facilities located (or might they be located at some future time) in the OE?

(6) How are CBRN materials brought to the OE?

(7) What are the generic and long-term effects of each CBRN hazard?

(8) What are reasonable expectations for completing assigned missions?

(9) Do any planning assumptions have to be changed?

(10) What approaches need to be changed to facilitate the development of viable COAs?

(11) What changes are there to the tactical environment and OE?

(12) What timelines will need to be changed?

(13) What organizational changes may need to be enacted?

(14) What are the operating forces' CBRN defense shortfalls and what can be done to mitigate these shortfalls?

f. Situational Understanding and Decision Making. Applying decisions based on the shared understanding of the CBRN situation also requires understanding when to deploy and employ CBRN defensive capabilities such as MOPP and COLPRO:

(1) Deploy CBRN Defense and Protection Assets. Deployment encompasses all activities from origin or home station through destination, specifically including not only movement legs, but also reception, staging, and onward movement/distribution. Examples of deployment decisions that might be needed:

(a) Where to deploy CBRN defense and protection assets?

(b) How much CBRN detection equipment to deploy?

(c) When to deploy CBRN medical assets?

(d) What type of CBRN decontamination materials to deploy?

(e) Has CBRN CM been tasked within the operational area, or should CBRN CM be anticipated during the assigned mission?

(2) Employ CBRN Defense and Protection Capabilities. Examples of employment decisions that may need to be made:

(a) Employ CBRN contamination mitigation assets.

(b) Employ CBRN defense medical assets.

(c) Employ CBRN reconstruction and stabilization assets.

(d) If directed, employ CBRN CM assets.

3. Protection

a. **General.** This discussion will focus on CBRN-related protection, not the general function of protection.

(1) Protection includes measures that conserve the force by identifying CBRN threats and hazards and preventing or mitigating the effects of CBRN environments. CBRN-related protection includes measures that are taken to keep CBRN environments from having an adverse effect on personnel, equipment, or critical assets and facilities. Protection planning is based on known or anticipated CBRN threats and hazards.

(2) Commanders implement protective measures appropriate to all anticipated threats, including terrorist threats and the use of WMD/CBRN or other sources of CBRN hazards. CBRN defense typically requires WMD active defense and CBRN passive defense and requires the planning, preparation, training, and execution of physical defenses to negate the effects of CBRN elements on personnel and materiel. MOPP gear for individuals and COLPRO systems provide protection in CBRN environments.

(3) As directed, the JFC's protection function may also extend beyond FP to encompass protection of US civilians; the forces, systems, and civil infrastructure of friendly nations; and other USG departments and agencies, IGOs, and NGOs.

(4) Protection capabilities for military forces against CBRN hazards also apply domestically. The Commander, United States Northern Command, or the Commander, United States Pacific Command, and subordinate commanders when tasked by the Secretary of Defense (SecDef) can apply protection capabilities during homeland defense, domestic CBRN CM for defense support of civil authorities, and for EP. National Guard forces have similar protections when functioning on state or federal active duty. DOD may be capable of preventing certain CBRN incidents during homeland defense, but DOD normally does not

have resources to provide individual protection or COLPRO for the general population against CBRN elements resulting from a CBRN incident.

b. WMD active defense includes measures to defeat an attack with WMD by employing actions to divert, neutralize, or destroy those weapons or their means of delivery while en route to their target. Throughout the operation or campaign, the JFC employs WMD active defense, CBRN passive defense, and other defensive capabilities. These are military-led activities (e.g., missile defense, air defense, and physical security) undertaken to defend against conventionally and asymmetrically delivered WMD. These capabilities should deny any benefit to the WMD threats and can influence an adversary's decisions to proliferate or employ WMD. These capabilities also represent benefits to allies and partners and can influence their support as well.

c. CBRN passive defense includes measures taken to minimize or negate the vulnerability to and effects of CBRN incidents. Protection is a principle of CBRN passive defense, which focuses on maintaining the joint force's ability to continue military operations in a CBRN environment. The JFC employs CBRN passive defense capabilities (e.g., integration of IPE and other equipment to protect against CBRN hazards, demonstrating to an adversary that personnel are trained) to reduce or negate vulnerabilities and minimize the effects of CBRN contamination. CBRN passive defense and other passive defense measures also protect US military interests, installations, and critical infrastructure. These capabilities also present benefits to other interagency and multinational partners and can influence their support as well.

For detailed information about execution of joint WMD active defense and CBRN passive defense, refer to JP 3-40, Countering Weapons of Mass Destruction. *For detailed information about tactical active and passive defense, refer to FM 3-11/MCWP 3-37.1/NWP 3-11/AFTTP 3-2.42,* Multi-Service Doctrine for CBRN Operations.

d. Emergency Management and CBRN Response Measures. Adversaries challenge FP capabilities at home stations even before deployment, through the threat of using CBRN weapons. Joint installation commanders manage and maintain comprehensive, all-hazards installation emergency management programs on DOD installations worldwide. Per DODI 6055.17, *DOD Installation Emergency Management (IEM) Program,* all hazards include any incident, natural or man-made, that warrants action to protect the life, property, health, and safety of military members, dependents, and civilians at risk, and minimize any disruptions of installation operations (including CBRN incidents). DOD maintains this capability for its installations and, as directed, supports and assists civil authorities in emergency management activities for mitigating, preventing, protecting, responding to, and recovering from natural or man-made CBRN incidents.

DODI 6055.17, DOD Installation Emergency Management (IEM) Program, *addresses requirements (including CBRN/hazardous materials) for responders within DOD. For further information, refer to ATP 3-11.42/MCWP 3-38.1/NTTP 3-11.36/AFTTP 3-2.83,* Multi-Service Tactics, Techniques, and Procedures for Installation Emergency Management.

4. Contamination Mitigation

a. **General.** Planning for contamination mitigation was discussed in Chapter II, "Planning and Preparation." As part of execution, contamination mitigation enables joint forces to sustain operations in a contaminated environment without prolonged interruption of OPTEMPO.

b. **Respond to Contamination.** The joint force quickly responds to contamination by initially mitigating the effects and performing only those actions required to allow continuation of the mission and, within mission constraints, save lives. The joint force applies contamination mitigation capabilities to maintain essential functions that must continue despite effects of hazardous contamination, or to enable the quick restoration of essential capabilities or combat power required to accomplish the current mission and achieve operational objectives. In some cases, as a result of automatic agent defeating capabilities, no additional joint force or individual actions are required. Only if directed should the joint force conduct CBRN CM in support of the civilian populations, to contribute to life saving and, as needed, maintain or restore essential services to support critical life-supporting activities.

c. **Recover from Contamination.** The joint force maintains military resources and capabilities to mitigate any hazardous contamination to recover/maintain unit readiness for the required range of mission activities at acceptable contamination levels.

d. **Contamination Control.** Contamination mitigation includes planning, initiating, and continuing operations despite the potential for CBRN hazards through the conduct of contamination control. A CBRN incident may contaminate essential operating areas. Local commanders need the capability to control the contamination, including the ability to decontaminate operating surfaces, materials handling equipment (MHE), aircraft, and exposed military cargo to the extent required to sustain operations. Large fixed sites (e.g., ports, airfields) with excess throughput capacity may allow split-MOPP operations implementation which provide the flexibility to shift operations to uncontaminated locations on the installation. At smaller facilities operating at 100 percent capacity, however, an incident could reduce throughput to a level below the JFC's requirements. Controlling contamination of equipment and operating surfaces at fixed sites is required to maintain operational capacity until restoration activities to unrestricted operations can be undertaken. The OPTEMPO and mission will determine the level of decontamination required.

For more information on decontamination operations and levels, see FM 3.11.5/MCWP 3-37.3/NTTP 3-11.26 /AFTTP(I) 3-2.60, Multi-Service Tactics, Techniques, and Procedures for Chemical, Biological, Radiological, and Nuclear Decontamination.

5. Sustainment Actions

a. **Sustainment Activities**

(1) The ability to sustain military combat operations with appropriate levels of logistics and personnel services is critical to operational success. JFC plans supporting RSOI

and sustainment must continually be reviewed. Operations in CBRN environments make sustainment planning more complex.

(2) OPTEMPO, logistic operations, health services, personnel services support, and reconstitution efforts may be profoundly affected by the introduction of CBRN hazards that present separate and distinct hazards to personnel, units, equipment, and operations.

(3) Generally, operations will slow as tasks are performed by personnel encumbered by protective equipment or exposed to CBRN environments which may require abandonment or only limited use of contaminated areas, transfer of missions to uncontaminated forces, or avoidance of contaminated terrain and routes. Additionally, use of WMD or other CBRN incidents resulting in a major disruption of normal personnel and materiel replacement processes in the theater could severely hamper the commanders' capabilities for force generation and sustainment.

(4) Split-MOPP options could make available many forces that would otherwise have been unavailable due to unnecessary protective level constraints. Force reconstitution requirements may also dramatically increase over initial planning estimates. Even when sufficient protection has been afforded to individuals and units, continued operations in a CBRN environment could overburden reorganization and reconstitution capabilities, as well as the deployed military health system capabilities.

b. **Logistics in Contaminated Environments.** Logistics are particularly vulnerable to CBRN incidents. For example, medical and sustainment supplies for quarantine/isolation facilities are time-sensitive. Inventory shortages of low-density CBRN protective equipment may require unplanned movement of these critical supplies. Personnel and equipment decontamination operations require large amounts of water, which creates large amounts of contaminated waste. These and other resources needed for recovery from CBRN incidents can severely strain the theater logistic system and caused unanticipated effects on combat operations.

c. **Post-Attack Reconnaissance.** Understanding the nature of CBRN contamination is central to adopting an effective concept of operations that reduces the risk of casualties and cross-contamination, and ensures the rapid resumption of operations after an incident. Coordinated reconnaissance, detection, identification, and marking is required. Personnel conduct self-assessment activities to detect possible contamination in their individual areas; however, military units trained and equipped to deal with CBRN contamination are normally necessary to support these CBRN surveys.

For more information, refer to ATP 3-11.37/MCWP 3-37.4/NTTP 3-11.29/AFTTP 3-2.44, Multi-Service Tactics, Techniques, and Procedures for Chemical, Biological, Radiological, and Nuclear Reconnaissance and Surveillance.

d. **Handling of Contaminated Materiel, Equipment, and Human Remains**

(1) Materiel and Equipment. The GCC is responsible for ensuring that all materiel and equipment exposed to CBRN contamination is decontaminated to clearance level before it is returned to stock or retrograded from the theater. Planning and Service TTP are used to

protect individuals against low-level CBRN hazard exposure, conserve valuable assets, identify requirements for the return of equipment and personnel to the US, and maintain DOD life cycle control of previously contaminated equipment. Due to the limitations of decontamination technology in meeting all safety and health standards, some contaminated equipment may require extensive weathering to meet safety standards. In some cases, equipment may be so grossly contaminated that reuse or repair is not practical and in-theater destruction may occur.

(a) In accordance with current publications, contaminated materiel and equipment that cannot be decontaminated for operational use is marked, segregated, and disposed of or decontaminated after the cessation of hostilities. Theater plans and orders provide guidance and procedures for retrograde of contaminated materiel and prioritize selected items that, due to their essential nature and short supply, require immediate retrograde, repair, and subsequent return to the theater. For retrograde of equipment via mobility air forces airlift, cargo will be decontaminated to a clearance level sufficient to prevent aircraft contamination.

(b) The length of time that nuclear and biological contaminants pose a health hazard is determined by their decay rates. The time required for the natural decay of radioactive material is a function of the half-life of the radionuclide and cannot be accelerated. If the residual radiation cannot be removed, commanders must employ the principles of time, distance, and shielding. Commanders should minimize the time that personnel are exposed to the radiation source; maximize the distance between personnel and the radiation source; and place as much shielding material, such as walls or soil, between personnel and the radiation source as possible. Biological agents generally decay to acceptable levels within hours after dissemination due to exposure to ultraviolet light (sunlight), relative humidity, wind speed, and temperature gradient. However, encapsulation or genetic engineering may protect agents from natural decay, increasing their persistency. For more robust biological agents, thorough decontamination and preparation of equipment to US Department of Agriculture import standards will eliminate most health threats.

(c) Equipment retrograde and redeployment requires valuable lift assets that must be protected from contamination for future use for moving forces. Only critical retrograde cargo should be moved from a contaminated location onto uncontaminated aviation and maritime lift assets. Critical requirements are designated in theater war plans. The intent to retrograde residually contaminated equipment must be communicated through the Chairman of the Joint Chiefs of Staff (CJCS) also due in part to potential foreign and domestic risks, and political/environmental sensitivities. The approval authority for landing contaminated aircraft at locations in areas outside of the continental US area or territory is coordinated through DOS and the HN. Requests for approval to land such aircraft will be made through the appropriate CCMD, which, in turn, will seek DOS approval. Requests for landing contaminated aircraft within the continental US or territories is coordinated by the Headquarters US Air Force/Deputy Chief of Staff for Plans and Operations, who will, in turn, seek DOD approval. DOD must coordinate with applicable civilian authorities, and will only issue guidance on contaminated aircraft movement after obtaining approval from the President or SecDef. CCDRs are responsible for cargo processing to include packaging, technical escort, reception and staging, foreign and interagency coordination; compliance with applicable US and international laws; compliance with treaties, conventions, and agreements to which the US is a party; and compliance with DOD policies on foreign and domestic CBRN CM.

(2) Human Remains. The GCC has the responsibility to search, recover, tentatively identify, and evacuate US human remains from the AOR. To complete this task, the JFC establishes a mortuary affairs contaminated remains mitigation site (MACRMS). This MACRMS is an operational element under the oversight of the joint mortuary affairs office (JMAO), and is manned by specialized mortuary affairs and CBRN personnel.

(a) In some circumstances the JFC may need to authorize alternative procedures for the disposition of human remains. If human remains cannot be decontaminated to a safe level, decontamination capabilities are not available, or for public health and safety, contaminated human remains may have to be temporarily interred or stored in a manner that contains the CBRN hazard and the location should be properly marked to facilitate contamination avoidance. In instances of mass fatalities, the JFC, on advice of the JMAO, may authorize temporary interment. The JMAO directs and controls subsequent disinterment. Temporary interments require dedicated transportation assets to avoid the spread of contamination, engineer support to prepare the site, and security personnel to prevent unauthorized personnel from entering the interment area.

(b) In accordance with DOD policy, USTRANSCOM transports human remains that have been properly decontaminated and rendered safe for transport in accordance with the procedures established in JP 4-06, *Mortuary Affairs*. However, contaminated human remains should remain in place and not be transported until such time as the methods for returning contaminated human remains safely have been established by SecDef.

For joint doctrine for handling contaminated human remains, see JP 4-06, Mortuary Affairs.

Intentionally Blank

CHAPTER IV
ASSESSMENT

1. Assessment

In the context of planning and executing military operations, assessment is a continuous process that measures the overall effectiveness of employing joint force capabilities. Assessment involves deliberately comparing forecast outcomes with actual events to determine the overall effectiveness of force employment. Specifically, an assessment process primarily helps the JFC and component commanders, and potentially other partners, determine progress toward accomplishing a task, creating a condition, or achieving an objective as the operation moves toward a desired end state. Assessment should not be confused with intelligence function providing intelligence assessments of the OE in the context of JIPOE. However, the intelligence function normally has major contributions to all levels of the assessment process of an operation or campaign. Assessments are applicable in all military operations. Based on their assessments, commanders direct adjustments, thus ensuring the operation remains focused on accomplishing the mission. Assessment of operations conducted in CBRN environments will increase the quantity and nature of variables that must be considered and analyzed to provide commanders with the most viable COAs. Planning and preparing for the assessment process must begin with the initial stage of joint operation planning, and during mission analysis, the initial set of mission success criteria normally becomes the basis for assessment. Assessment considerations help guide operational design because they can affect the sequence and type of actions along lines of operation and lines of effort.

2. Assessment Process

The assessment process is directly tied to the commander's decision cycle throughout planning, preparation, and execution of operations. It entails three distinct tasks: continuously monitoring the situation and the progress of the operations; evaluating the operation against measures of effectiveness (MOEs) and measures of performance (MOPs) to determine progress relative to the mission, objectives, and end states; and developing recommendations and/or guidance for improvement.

a. Staffs help the commanders by monitoring the numerous aspects that can influence the outcome of operations and providing the commander timely information needed for decisions. The assessment process approved by the commander helps the staff by identifying and monitoring key aspects of the operation that the commander is interested in and where the commander wants to make decisions.

b. Normally, the operations directorate of a joint staff or the plans directorate of a joint staff, assisted by the intelligence directorate of a joint staff, is responsible for coordinating assessment activities. For subordinate commanders' staffs, this may be accomplished by equivalent elements within Service and/or joint functional components.

c. During planning, the staff analyzes threats, hazards, vulnerabilities, and capabilities to assist commanders in determining and refining priorities, task organization decisions, logistics and health services, intelligence collection requirements, resource allocation, and readiness requirements. The assessment process should identify activities required to maintain situational awareness, monitor and evaluate staff estimates and tasks, develop and monitor MOEs and MOPs, and identify potential variances that could require decisions.

d. During execution, the staff monitors and evaluates the progress of current operations to validate assumptions made in planning and to continually update changes to the situation. The staff also monitors the conduct of operations, looking for variances. When variances exceed threshold values developed or directed in planning, the staff may recommend an adjustment, such as an order to counter an unanticipated CBRN threat or hazard or to mitigate a developing vulnerability. They also track the status of assets and evaluate their effectiveness as they are employed.

e. The staff should monitor and evaluate the following aspects of the CBRN environment as part of the assessment process:

    (1) Changes to CBRN threats and hazards.

    (2) Changes in CBRN force vulnerabilities.

    (3) Changes to unit capabilities.

    (4) Validity of assumptions as they pertain to CBRN defense.

    (5) Staff and commander estimates.

    (6) CBRN environments and their conditions and changes.

    (7) CBRN resource allocations.

    (8) Increased risks.

    (9) Supporting efforts.

For additional information on the overall assessment process, see JP 5-0, Joint Operation Planning.

APPENDIX A
CHEMICAL HAZARD CONSIDERATIONS

1. General

Exposure to toxic chemicals can significantly influence the OPTEMPO and sustainment of forces. This appendix presents a brief overview of chemical agents and TICs and their effects. The following definitions are important in understanding this overview.

a. **Chemical Hazard.** Any chemical manufactured, used, transported, or stored, which can cause death, harm the environment, or cause other harm through toxic properties of those materials, including chemical agents and chemical weapons (prohibited under the CWC) as well as TICs.

b. **Chemical Warfare Agent (CWA) or Chemical Agents.** A chemical substance which is intended for use in military operations to kill, seriously injure, or incapacitate mainly through its physiological effects. The term excludes riot control agents when used for law enforcement purposes, herbicides, smoke, and flames.

c. **Chemical Weapon.** Together or separately:

(1) A toxic chemical and its precursors, except when intended for a purpose not prohibited under the CWC.

(2) A munition or device, specifically designed to cause death or other harm through toxic properties of those chemicals described in paragraph (1) above, which would be released as a result of the employment of such munition or device.

(3) Any equipment specifically designed for use directly in connection with the employment of munitions or devices described in paragraph (2) above.

d. Military chemical compounds (other than CWAs). These are chemical compounds that are developed, in part, for military use (riot control agents and obscurants), but not as weapons. Toxic properties are primarily associated with improper use.

e. **TIC.** Any hazardous chemical manufactured, used, transported, or stored by industrial, medical, or commercial processes. For example: pesticides, petrochemicals, fertilizers, corrosives, or poisons.

2. Chemical Agents

a. Chemical agents are classified as nerve, choking, blood, blister, and incapacitating agents. The terms "persistent" and "nonpersistent" describe the time an agent stays in an area. Persistent chemical agents affect the contaminated area for more than 24 hours to several days or weeks. Conversely, a nonpersistent agent normally dissipates and/or loses its ability to cause casualties after considerably less time, but is usually a more lethal agent. The effects on personnel exposed to these hazards may be immediate or delayed. A summary of effects for persistent and nonpersistent chemical agents is shown in Figure A-1.

Chemical Agent Effects

Persistency	Target of Choice	Target Effect
Nonpersistent • Nerve • Blood • Choking	• Personnel	• Immediate • Lethal
Persistent • Nerve • Blister	• Terrain • Materiel • Logistics • Command and control facilities	• Reduced operations tempo or mission degradation • Lethal or casualty producing

Figure A-1. Chemical Agent Effects

b. Figure A-2 indicates individual symptoms and effects, rate of action, and how chemical agents are normally disseminated.

c. Adversaries will seek to employ chemical agents under favorable weather conditions, if possible, to increase their effectiveness. Weather factors considered are wind, air stability, temperature, humidity, and precipitation. **Note: Adversaries may not wait for favorable weather conditions to employ chemical agents in order to create their desired effects.**

d. Adversaries may choose to deliver agents upwind of targets; in which case, stable or neutral conditions with low to medium winds of 5-13 kilometers per hour (kph) are the most favorable conditions. Marked turbulence, winds above 13 kph, moderate to heavy rain, or an air stability category of "unstable" result in unfavorable conditions for chemical clouds. However, the adversary may be able to leverage these factors to effectively employ a persistent agent to contaminate water supplies, deny terrain, material, etc.

e. Most weather conditions do not affect the quantity of munitions needed for effective, initial liquid contamination.

f. The Defense Threat Reduction Agency (DTRA) reachback can help to identify further information on the impact of the environment on chemical agent dispersion (see Appendix F, "Technical Chemical, Biological, Radiological, and Nuclear Forces," paragraph 6, for DTRA Operations Center contact information).

3. **Toxic Industrial Chemicals**

a. US forces frequently operate in environments in which TICs are present. A number of these chemicals could interfere in a significant manner across the range of military

Classes of Chemical Warfare Agents

Types	Symptoms	Effects	Rate of Action	Release Form
Nerve	• difficulty breathing • sweating • drooling • nausea • vomiting • convulsions • dimming of vision • headache • (symptoms usually develop quickly)	• incapacitates at low concentrations • death at high concentrations	• very rapid by inhalation or through the eyes • slower through the skin	• aerosol • vapor • liquid
Blood Choking	• difficulty breathing • coma	• interference with respiration at cellular level or by interfering with oxygen transport	• rapid	• aerosol • vapor
Blister	• symptoms range from immediate to delayed (agent dependent) • searing of eyes • stinging of skin • powerful irritation of eyes, nose, and skin	• blisters skin and respiratory tract • can cause temporary blindness • some sting and form welts on the skin	• blisters from mustard may appear several hours after exposure • Lewisite causes prompt burning, redness within 30 minutes; blister on first and second days • phosgene oxime causes immediate, intense pain	• liquid • particulate

Figure A-2. Classes of Chemical Warfare Agents

operations. Most TICs of immediate concern are released as vapors. These vapors exhibit the same dissemination characteristics as CWAs. The vapors tend to remain concentrated in natural low-lying areas such as valleys, ravines, or man-made underground structures downwind from the release point. High concentrations may remain in buildings, woods, or areas with low air circulation. Explosions may spread liquid hazards and vapors may condense to liquids in cold air.

b. Figure A-3 identifies recommended isolation and protective action distances associated with accidental releases of some selected TICs, as recommended by the *Emergency Response Guidebook* (ERG). Isolation and protective action distances listed in

Industrial Chemical Site Minimum Downwind Hazard (Sample)

Chemical*	Small Release (< 55 Gallon Drum)			Large Release (> 55 Gallons or Multiple Small Releases)		
	Isolate All Directions (Meters)	Protect Downwind (Kilometers)		Isolate All Directions (Meters)	Protect Downwind (Kilometers)	
		Day	Night		Day	Night
Ammonia	60	0.2	0.2	120	1.2	4.4
Chlorine	60	0.4	2.4	480	2.4	7.4
Nitric Acid	60	0.2	0.2	120	1.2	2.4
Phosgene	180	1.8	8.2	1600	6.6	21+
Sulfuric Acid	120	0.8	2.0	660	5	13
Hydrochloric Acid						
Petrochemicals	As an immediate precautionary measure, isolate release in all directions for at least 50 meters for liquids and at least 25 meters for solids.					
Phosphoric Acid						

* Samples only. See the current version of the *Emergency Response Guidebook* for additional information.

Figure A-3. Industrial Chemical Site Minimum Downwind Hazard (Sample)

the ERG apply to a terrorist or insurgent release of TICs. If the quantity of the TIC released is unknown, the distances for the large spills in the ERG should be utilized. Release of TICs is most dangerous at night. The downwind hazard from a nighttime release is much longer because of cooler temperature and less wind than during the daytime.

Note: Distances in Figure A-3 are worst case scenarios involving the instantaneous release of the entire contents of a package (e.g., as a result of terrorism, sabotage, or catastrophic accident). Figure A-3 distances were obtained by multiplying US Department of Transportation ERG distances by a factor of two.

c. The most important action in case of an industrial chemical release is **immediate evacuation from the hazard's path.** The greatest risk from a large-scale toxic chemical release occurs when personnel are unable to escape the immediate area and are overcome by vapors or blast effects. **Military respirators and protective clothing may provide only**

limited protection against TICs but should be used, if available, during the immediate evacuation from the hazard area if more appropriate protective gear is not available.

d. In planning for operations in areas that might include TICs, commanders at all levels should include consideration of these potential hazards as part of the JIPOE process. These hazards could occur from deliberate or accidental release from industrial sites as well as storage and transport containers. It is possible that enemies could use an improvised explosive device (IED) to disperse TICs. Particular emphasis should be placed on those TICs that produce acute effects when inhaled or that produce large amounts of toxic vapor when spilled in water. The findings from a comprehensive TIC assessment provide the risks presented by TIC in an OE.

For detailed information on these and other TIC hazards, see the National Institute for Occupational Safety and Health Pocket Guide to Chemical Hazards, *the US Department of Transportation* ERG, and the US National Library of Medicine Toxicology Data Network at http://toxnet.nlm.nih.gov/.

Intentionally Blank

APPENDIX B
BIOLOGICAL HAZARD CONSIDERATIONS

1. General

Militarily significant characteristics for biological aspects of operations include: a normally vulnerable target population; contagious or toxic agents with highly lethal or incapacitating properties; agent availability or adaptability for scaled-up production; agent stability; and agent suitability for mass dispersion. Limiting factors include biological properties (e.g., virulence), environmental factors (e.g., ultraviolet light causing rapid decay), and dissemination methods (e.g., wet versus dry aerosol).

2. Technical Aspects

a. Biological agents are microorganisms capable of causing disease in humans, livestock, and agriculture. Biological hazards are organisms, or substances derived from an organism, that pose a threat to human, plant, or animal health. These hazards include medical wastes, microorganisms, viruses, or toxins (from a biological source). Pathogens are disease-producing microorganisms (for example, bacteria, viruses, rickettsia, prions) that directly attack human, plant, or animal tissue and biological processes. Pathogens are further divided into noncontagious or contagious. When biological hazards are contagious, planning needs to account for possible quarantines and evacuations. Toxins are nonliving poisonous substances that are produced naturally by living organisms (e.g., plants, animals, insects, bacteria, fungi) but may also be synthetically manufactured. These hazards can originate from sources such as medical waste and biological environmental samples and/or clinical specimens. Advances in biotechnology, genetic engineering, and natural mutation may facilitate the development or emergence of deadlier BW agents. BW is the employment of biological agents to produce casualties in personnel, livestock, and animals or damage to plants and materiel; or defense against such employment. Figure B-1 provides a list of selected BW agents and their disease characteristics.

(1) The ability to modify microbial agents at a molecular (gene) level has existed since the 1960s, when new genetic engineering techniques were introduced, but the enterprise tended to be slow and unpredictable. With today's techniques, infectious organisms can be modified to become more infectious and resistant to current prophylaxis and treatment options, or to exhibit novel disease characteristics. The current level of sophistication for many biological agents is low, but there is enormous potential—based on advances in modern molecular biology and drug delivery technology—for making more sophisticated weapons. BW agents may emerge in two likely categories: man-made manipulations of classic BW agents and newly discovered or emerging infectious diseases. An example of a recent new pathogen (though not necessarily an ideal BW agent) is *Streptococcus pneumoniae* S23F, a naturally occurring strain of bacteria resistant to at least six of the more commonly used antibiotics.

Pathogens, Viruses, and Toxins of Military Significance

Disease	Routes of Infection	Untreated Mortality (%)	Incubation Period	Vaccine	Transmissibility (Human to Human)
Bacteria and Rickettsia					
Anthrax (*Bacillus anthracis*)	S, R C, I	S: 5-20 R: 80-90	1-4 Days	Yes	No
Plague (*Yersinia pestis*)	V, R	60	2-3 Days	No	High
Q Fever (*Cociella burnetti*)	V, R	< 1	2-10 Days	IND	No
Tularemia (*Francisella tularensis*)	D, V, R	30-60	2-10 Days	IND	No
Viruses					
Smallpox (*Variola major*)	R	30	10-12 Days	Available (controlled US stock)	High
Viral equine encephalitis (e.g., Western, Eastern, Venezuelan)	R, V	< 1	2-6 Days	IND	Low
Viral hemorrhagic fevers (Ebola, Marburg, Lassa, Rift Valley, Dengue, etc.)	DC, R, V	Up to 90 (virus dependent)	3-21 Days	No	Moderate
Toxins					
Botulism (*Botulinum neurotoxins*)	D, R	60	1-4 Days	IND: (available only under FDA-approved protocol)	No
Ricin (*Ricinus communis*)	D, R	30	Hours to Days	No	No
Staphylococcal Enterotoxin B	D, R	< 1	Hours to Days	No	No
Trichothecene Mycotoxins (T2)	D, R, S	10-60	—	No	Yes (from skin contact)

NOTE:
Cutaneous in this context refers to a break in the skin. A vector is any organism that carries and transmits an infectious pathogen.

Legend

C cutaneous
D digestive system
DC direct contact
FDA Food and Drug Administration
I ingestion
IND investigational new drug
R respiratory system
S skin
V vector

Figure B-1. Pathogens, Viruses, and Toxins of Military Significance

(2) The types of modified biological agents that could potentially be produced through genetic engineering methodologies are listed below. Each of these techniques seeks to capitalize on the extreme lethality, virulence, or infectivity of BW agents and exploit this potential by developing methods to deliver agents more efficiently and to gain control of the agent on the battlefield.

(a) Benign microorganisms genetically altered to produce a toxin or bioregulator (naturally occurring organic compounds that regulate diverse cellular processes in multiple organ systems, such as heart rate).

(b) Microorganisms resistant to antibiotics, standard vaccines, antivirals, and therapeutics.

(c) Microorganisms with enhanced aerosol and environmental stability.

(d) Immunologically altered microorganisms able to defeat standard detection, identification, and diagnostic methods.

(e) Combinations of the above four types with improved delivery systems.

b. **Toxic Industrial Biological (TIB).** TIBs include infectious agents, as well as other biological hazards. The risk can be direct through infection or indirect through damage to the environment. TIBs are often generated as infectious waste, such as on sharp-edged medical instruments commonly known as "sharps" (e.g., needles, syringes, and lancets) and material contaminated by bodily fluids, and as biological clinical specimens (e.g., biopsies, diseases for research).

3. Operational Considerations

a. **Dissemination.** Biological agents may be dispersed or deposited as aerosols, liquid droplets, or dry powders. In general, agents dispersed as dry powder are more viable than those dispersed as wet aerosols. Biological agents can also be transmitted directly by arthropod vectors or by an infected individual. An arthropod is an invertebrate animal having an exoskeleton. Infected arthropod vectors are useful for penetrating the skin.

b. **Persistency.** The longevity of biological agents is greatly dependent on their viability (ability to cause disease). Examples of viability are shown in Figure B-2.

c. **Environmental Conditions.** Environmental conditions may also affect the viability of biological material (see Figure B-3). These conditions include: solar (ultraviolet) radiation, relative humidity, wind speed, and temperature gradient. Ultraviolet light decreases the viability of most aerosol disseminated biological agents. However, encapsulation through man-made processes, natural sporulation, or arthropod vectors, may protect biological agents from the impacts of the environment and increase agent viability.

d. **Trigger Events.** With current technology, it is possible that a BW attack will occur before local commanders are aware that it has taken place. Commanders, in conjunction with their medical staffs, must attempt to distinguish between an epidemic of natural origin,

Examples of Biological Material Viability

Disease	Likely Dissemination Method	Infectivity	Lethality	Viability
Bacteria and Rickettsia				
Anthrax (*Bacillus anthracis*)	Spores in aerosol	Moderate	High	Spores Are Highly Stable
Plague (*Yersinia pestis*)	• Aerosol • Vectors	High	Very High	Less Important Because of High Transmissibility
Q Fever (*Cociella burnetti*)	• Aerosol • Sabotage (food)	High	Very Low	Stable
Tularemia (*Francisella tularensis*)	• Aerosol • Sabotage (food, water) • Vectors	High	Moderate	Not Very Stable
Viruses				
Smallpox (Variola Major)	Aerosol	High	High	Stable
Viral equine encephalitis (e.g., Western, Eastern, Venezuelan)	Aerosol	High	Low	Relatively Unstable
Viral hemorrhagic fevers (Ebola, Marburg, Lassa, Rift Valley, Dengue, etc.)	Aerosol	High	High - Low (Virus Dependent)	Relatively Stable
Toxins				
Botulism (*Botulinum neurotoxins*)	• Aerosol • Sabotage	N/A	High	Stable
Ricin (*Ricinus communis*)	Aerosol	N/A	Moderate	Stable
Staphylococcal Enterotoxin B	• Aerosol • Sabotage	N/A	Low	Stable

Figure B-2. Examples of Biological Material Viability

a BW attack, or the release of/exposure to TIBs. Trigger events can assist commanders and the medical staff by providing an indication that a BW event is likely to occur, may have occurred, or has occurred, and will prompt commanders to initiate response measures. Possible triggers signaling a biological event include: intelligence indicators generally occur prior to an event; weapons and detector triggers indicate agent release and/or disease infection start times; and a sentinel casualty trigger identifies the onset of symptoms.

Weather Effects on Biological Agent Dissemination

	Weather Condition	Biological Warfare Agent Cloud Performance	Operational Considerations
Favorable	Stable or inversion conditions	Agent clouds travel downwind for long distances before they spread laterally. High humidity and light rains generally favor wet agent dissemination.	Agent clouds tend to dissipate uniformly and remain cohesive as they travel downwind. Clouds lie low to the ground and may not rise high enough to cover the tops of buildings and/or other tall objects.
Marginal	Neutral conditions	Agent clouds tend to dissipate quickly.	More agent required for the same results as under stable conditions. Desired results may not be achieved.
Unfavorable	Unstable or lapse conditions	Agent clouds rise rapidly and do not travel downwind any appreciable distance. Cold temperatures affect wet agent dissemination.	Agent clouds tend to break up and become diffused. Little operational benefit from off-target dissemination.

Figure B-3. Weather Effects on Biological Agent Dissemination

See DODI 6200.03, Public Health Emergency Management Within the Department of Defense, *for further description of roles, responsibilities, and qualifications of medical staff.*

(1) Intelligence warning trigger events occur when a commander receives convincing information (unanalyzed) or intelligence (analyzed information) indicating that a biological event (naturally occurring, accidental, or intentional) is imminent. Information and intelligence from multiple sources (e.g., the general public, military intelligence, national intelligence institutions in the host country) can provide advance warning of a biological event.

(2) Weapons event trigger events refer to attacks by a weapon system(s), such as theater ballistic missile(s), artillery, or observed attacks employing other delivery means such as an aerosol sprayer device. Where intelligence has assessed a biological weapon

capability, it is reasonable to initially react to weapons events as if they could contain biological agents.

(3) Detector alarm trigger events refer to the discovery of a biological event via a positive result from a detection device, positive identification of environmental samples (i.e., water, food), indicating that a biological agent is present. Detectors are not a foolproof method of indicating the presence of biological agents due to the sensitivity threshold limitations of the devices and the possibility of false negatives/positives. Positive results via detector, followed up with laboratory analysis, may permit discovery of a biological hazard prior to the onset of symptoms.

(4) A sentinel casualty trigger event refers to the medical community's detection of a biological agent or infectious disease hazard by assessing trends in medical symptoms among personnel or diagnosis of an index case. Response actions based on a sentinel casualty may begin well into the disease progression cycle. This information may be made available via the news media, the Centers for Disease Control and Prevention, the Armed Forces Health Surveillance Center, the Service's public health centers, the World Health Organization, or state and local public health departments.

e. **Additional Attack Indicators.** In addition to the trigger events listed in paragraph 3d, "Trigger Events," the surrounding environment can also provide indication of a BW attack. Particular attention should be given to the following:

(1) Increased numbers of sick or dead animals, often of different species. Some BW agents are capable of infecting/intoxicating a wide range of hosts.

(2) Unusual entomological parameters (dead insects).

f. **Sources and Requirements for Weaponization.** Very little distinguishes a vaccine or pharmaceutical plant from a BW production facility. Nearly all the equipment, technology, and materials needed for BW agent production are dual use. On a smaller scale, the same type of equipment is found in research facilities and universities as well. However, the means of production is directly tied to the means of dissemination. Far less technical production capability is required in order to produce a BW to disseminate in an IED or letter than it is for a ballistic missile.

For additional information on BW development, production, and weaponization, see The Worldwide Biological Warfare Weapons Threat *(http://www.dia.smil.mil/intel/nuke/ bio/biowar.pdf).*

4. Biological Defense

Biological defense comprises the methods, plans, and procedures involved in establishing and executing defensive measures against biological attack. In striking contrast to protection against chemical, radiological, and nuclear weapons there exists the potential to minimize the effects of biological agents. The combined use of medical surveillance, identification, medical countermeasures, physical protection, and ROM provides the basis of biological defense.

a. **Medical Surveillance**. In some cases, human beings may be the only biodetector. Early clinical findings may be nonspecific or atypical of the natural disease. Medical personnel may be unable to differentiate natural disease from BW attacks. Considerable time may elapse following a BW attack before the extent of the exposure is known. To enable identification of a BW attack, ongoing, systematic collection and analysis of health data are essential. Following a BW attack, the disease pattern may have characteristics that differ from those of a naturally occurring epidemic. The following are examples:

(1) In contrast to naturally occurring epidemics (excluding food-borne outbreaks) in which disease incidence increases over a period of weeks or months, the epidemic curve for most large, artificially induced outbreaks is compressed, peaking within a few hours or days.

(2) In contrast to the peaks and troughs evident in most natural disease outbreaks, a steady and increasing stream of patients may be seen (comparable to that during an accidental food poisoning outbreak).

(3) An understanding of disease ecology and epidemiology can be extremely useful in distinguishing natural outbreaks from those induced by BW attack. For example, diseases that are naturally vector-borne will have environmental parameters that predispose to naturally occurring outbreaks. Appearance of disease in the absence of these parameters would be highly suggestive of a BW attack.

(4) The military health system must maintain routine disease surveillance; emergence of an atypical pattern mandates immediate notification of higher authority. The simultaneous appearance of outbreaks in different geographical locations should alert to the possibility of a BW attack. In addition, multiple biological agents may be used simultaneously in a BW attack, or chemical and biological agents may be combined in a single attack to complicate diagnosis.

(5) A large number of casualties within a period of 48-72 hours (suggesting an attack with a microorganism), or within hours (suggesting an attack with a toxin). The epidemiology would be that of a massive single source.

(6) A large number of clinical cases among exposed individuals.

(7) An illness type highly unusual for the geographic area (e.g., Venezuelan equine encephalitis [VEE] in Europe).

(8) An illness occurring in an unnatural epidemiological setting, where environmental parameters are not conducive to natural transmission (e.g., VEE in the absence of antecedent disease in horses or in the absence of vector mosquitoes). (Epidemiology is the branch of medicine that deals with the study of the causes, distribution, and control of disease in populations.)

(9) An unusually high prevalence of respiratory involvement in diseases that when acquired in nature, generally cause a non-pulmonary syndrome—the signature of aerosol exposure (e.g., inhalational anthrax).

(10) Casualty distribution aligned with recent wind direction.

(11) Lower attack rates among those working indoors, especially in areas with filtered air or closed ventilation systems, than in those exposed outdoors. The reverse is true when the attack is made by using ventilation systems in order to disseminate BW agents indoors.

(12) Large numbers of rapidly fatal cases, with few recognizable signs and symptoms, resulting from exposure to multiple lethal doses near the dissemination source.

b. **Identification**

(1) There are four levels of identification associated with CBRN hazards. The higher the level of identification, the higher confidence the commander has that a CBRN incident has occurred. The four levels are:

(a) Presumptive identification is the employment of technologies with limited specificity and sensitivity, by conventional forces in a field environment to determine the presence of a CBRN hazard with a low level of confidence and the degree of certainty necessary to support immediate tactical decisions.

(b) Field confirmatory identification is the employment of technologies with increased specificity and sensitivity by technical forces in a field environment to identify CBRN hazards with a moderate level of confidence and the degree of certainty necessary to support follow-on tactical decisions.

(c) Theater validation identification is the employment of multiple independent, established protocols and technologies by scientific experts in the controlled environment of a fixed or mobile/transportable laboratory to characterize a CBRN hazard with a high level of confidence and the degree of certainty necessary to support operational-level decisions.

(d) Definitive identification is the employment of multiple state-of-the-art, independent, established protocols and technologies by scientific experts in a nationally recognized laboratory to determine the unambiguous identity of a CBRN hazard with the highest level of confidence and degree of certainty necessary to support strategic-level decisions.

(2) Identification of BW agents is essential to determine appropriate operational and medical countermeasure responses that may be taken by the JFC and public health officials.

(a) Presumptive identification of the BW agent in the operational area will influence initial responses. BW agent categories can generally be described as:

1. Communicable diseases, such as pneumonic plague, smallpox, influenza, and many others, that are able to be transmitted from person to person.

<u>2.</u> Noncommunicable diseases, such as anthrax, that can contaminate an area and infect personnel but are not able to be transmitted from person to person.

<u>3.</u> Noncommunicable BW agents, such as toxins and many other bacterial pathogens, that primarily only cause effects in directly exposed personnel.

(b) Field confirmatory identification is obtained using fielded devices/materials/technologies available to specially trained personnel and units in a field environment that includes collections and analyses of samples to substantiate the presence and type of a biological substance at a given location. Field confirmatory identification can be used to prove (or disprove) previous presumptive results. It results in higher confidence levels to support tactical decisions regarding avoidance, protection, and decontamination measures and immediate treatment.

(c) Theater validation identification qualifies a biological sample if using the accepted quality assurance measures. It provides additional critical information to support timely and effective decisions regarding avoidance, protection, decontamination measures, medical prophylaxis, and treatment for affected units and personnel. It can also support preliminary attribution to implicate or support trace analytics for the source of the identified CBRN material.

c. **Medical Countermeasures**

(1) **Immunoprophylaxis**

(a) **Active Immunoprophylaxis.** Vaccination is an important practical means of providing continuous protection against BW hazards prior to, as well as during, hostile actions. Vaccines against a number of potential BW agents are available. Many of these vaccines were developed for the protection of laboratory workers or individuals working where the target diseases are endemic.

<u>1.</u> During a BW agent attack the number of infectious or toxin units to which an individual is exposed may be greater than in the case of natural exposure. Exposure by inhalation may represent an unnatural route of infection with many BW agents. The efficacy afforded by most vaccines is based on route of exposure and presentation of disease. Vaccines, which are generally considered to be effective under natural circumstances, may not provide a similar degree of protection to individuals exposed to aerosolized or genetically altered agents.

<u>2.</u> An appropriate immunization policy is essential. Vaccines are biological agent-specific and do not provide immediate protection. Not all vaccines can be administered simultaneously; therefore to prevent the logistic problems caused by in-theater vaccination, prior immunization is essential.

<u>3.</u> If an in-theater vaccination program is required, the possibility of adverse reactions from vaccination and the concomitant degradation of operational efficiency should be taken into account.

(b) **Passive Immunoprophylaxis.** For some biological agents, the only available medical countermeasures might be specific antiserum. Under certain conditions, passive immunoprophylaxis with immunoglobulin products might be considered. Use may be limited by lack of adequate sources and quantities of material, limited duration of protection, and the risk of serum sickness associated with antisera of animal origin. However, recent scientific advances in products for immunoprophylaxis (for example, human monoclonal antibodies, despeciated equine or ovine antisera) are making this option technically more attractive.

(2) **Chemoprophylaxis**

(a) Chemoprophylaxis using appropriate drugs (e.g., antibacterials, antibiotics, antivirals) may offer additional protection in the event of a BW incident. If an attack is felt to be imminent (i.e., intelligence indicator), or is known to have occurred (i.e., weapon event or a sentinel casualty), command-directed chemoprophylaxis would be appropriate for all personnel in the area. However, it is impractical and wasteful to place everyone located in a potential target area on prolonged, routine antimicrobial prophylaxis in the absence of such a threat condition.

(b) For bacterial agents, antibiotics should be administered as soon as possible following exposure. Initiation of chemoprophylaxis during the incubation period is always worthwhile; however, the earlier the antibiotic is given the greater is the chance of preventing disease. In some cases (e.g., inhalational anthrax), post-exposure vaccination must be given in addition to antibiotics to personnel previously unvaccinated to prevent late onset of disease when antibiotics are withdrawn.

(c) Consideration should be given to the possibility of the interaction between drugs in multi-drug regimens that address the multiple elements of force health protection. Medical personnel must ensure consistent observation of personnel receiving chemoprophylaxis in order to identify and treat harmful interactions or side effects.

d. **Physical Protection**

(1) **IPE/PPE**

(a) **Respiratory Protection.** Respiratory protection is essential in the presence of any BW inhalation hazard. Currently fielded respirators equipped with standard filter canisters will provide a high degree of protection. Other forms of protection (e.g., self-contained breathing apparatus) are available and may be fielded to meet particular conditions. Low-grade masks (e.g., surgical masks) are not sufficient to protect against aerosol attacks. However, they may have some application for controlling the spread of contagious disease. Personnel using military and/or commercial protective equipment (e.g., military protective masks, commercial respirators, military and commercial protective clothing) shall be required to follow Service-specific PPE requirements.

(b) **Dermal Protection.** Intact skin provides an excellent barrier against biological agents; however, any skin abrasions or inflammation must be covered. In some instances it may be necessary to protect the mucous membranes of the eye. IPE clothing employed against CBRN agents will protect against skin contamination with biological agents, although standard uniform clothing affords a certain degree of protection against dermal exposure to the surfaces covered.

(c) **Casualties.** Casualties unable to continue wearing IPE in a biological agent contaminated area should be held and/or transported using containment measures to protect the casualty against biological agent exposure. Contagious patients should be held and/or transported using a barrier system to prevent disease transmission.

(2) **COLPRO**

(a) A COLPRO shelter is a dedicated hardened or unhardened shelter equipped with a CBRN air filtration unit. This shelter provides an overpressure environment to allow medical treatment personnel to work inside with minimal IPE/PPE or without the need for additional IPE/PPE. Contaminated patients, staff, and equipment/materials must be decontaminated prior to entering a COLPRO shelter in order to maintain its integrity.

(b) COLPRO is the most effective method for protecting clean patients, medical personnel, and the medical treatment facility (MTF) during the primary BW attack. Patients whose illness is thought to be the result of a BW attack or those who are thought to have a transmissible disease, will necessarily be cared for using barrier protection techniques. The environment within COLPRO may promote cross-infection between casualties and staff and it may be appropriate to care for these patients outside COLPRO.

For more information on individual, patient, and caregiver protection, refer to FM 4-02.7/MCRP 4-11.1F/NTTP 4-02.7/AFTTP 3-42.3, Multi-Service Tactics, Techniques, and Procedures for Health Service Support in a Chemical, Biological, Radiological, and Nuclear Environment.

e. **ROM, Isolation, and Quarantine.** To prevent the spread of an infectious disease or contagious illness, public health authorities use different strategies. ROM, isolation, and quarantine enforcement actions are generally within the jurisdiction of the state and local authorities. Enforcement actions by DOD personnel will likely be restricted by the Posse Comitatus Act and/or DOD policy unless an alternative statutory or constitutional authority exists (e.g., Presidential invocation of the Insurrection Act). Three of these strategies are ROM, isolation, and quarantine.

(1) ROM refers to potentially infected persons and the restriction of their movement to stop the spread of that illness. Restrictions of movement may be implemented to prevent the spread of contagious diseases. In the case of military personnel, restrictions of movement, including isolation or quarantine, or any other measure necessary to prevent or limit transmitting a communicable disease may be implemented. In the case of persons other than military personnel, restrictions of movement may include limiting ingress to, egress from, or movement on a military installation.

(2) Isolation refers to the separation of persons who have a specific infectious illness from a healthy population. Isolation allows for the target delivery of specialized medical care to people who are ill, while protecting healthy people from getting sick.

Infected people in isolation may be cared for in their homes, in hospitals, or in designated MTFs. DODI 6200.03, *Public Health Emergency Management Within the Department of Defense,* addresses requirements (including ROM) for managing the impact of public health emergencies caused by all hazards incidents.

(3) Quarantine refers to the separation and ROM of persons who, while not yet ill and have not shown signs and symptoms of the disease, have been exposed to an infectious agent and therefore may become infectious. Quarantine involves the confinement and active, continued health surveillance of an individual who is suspected of having been exposed to an infectious agent until determined that they are free of infection. Quarantine is medically very effective in protecting the public from disease.

APPENDIX C
NUCLEAR HAZARD CONSIDERATIONS

1. General

The international security environment encompasses threats from potential adversaries armed with nuclear weapons. This appendix summarizes common effects produced by nuclear weapons, high-energy radiation, and radiological materials to assist combatant and subordinate commanders to plan for and conduct operations in nuclear environments. The effects of radiation exposure described in Appendix D, "Radiological Hazard Considerations," also apply to the residual radiation including fallout from a nuclear explosion.

2. Characteristics of Nuclear Weapons

a. The nature and intensity of the effects (especially height of burst) of a nuclear detonation depend upon the characteristics of the weapon and the target and the means of employment. The most significant characteristics of a nuclear weapon are its type and yield.

b. **Types of Nuclear Weapons.** Nuclear weapons release enormous amounts of energy liberated from the fission or fusion of atomic nuclei. Fission-based weapons utilize specific isotopes of massive elements, such as uranium or plutonium, as the fuel for the fission reactions. Fission-based weapons are often configured as gun-type weapons. Because these weapons require a relatively lower level of technological sophistication, they are more likely to be developed or used by underdeveloped nations or terrorist groups. Fusion-based weapons exploit the energy released when the nuclei of light elements, such as isotopes of hydrogen, combine to form more massive nuclei and are often referred to as hydrogen bombs or H-bombs. Fusion-based weapons require very high temperatures to enable fusion reactions and may also be referred to as thermonuclear weapons. Since fusion-based weapons require much greater technological sophistication and are more efficient, more technologically mature nations are likely to adopt this weapon type.

c. **Yield.** The term yield is used to describe the amount of explosive energy released when a nuclear weapon is detonated. A nuclear weapon's yield is measured in units of tons of TNT (trinitrotoluene) that would produce an equivalent explosion. Fission-based weapons are capable of producing yields up to a few hundred kilotons (kt). Thermonuclear weapons can produce yields in excess of 25 megatons.

3. Nuclear Weapons Effects

a. The effects of a nuclear weapon are largely determined by the medium in which it is detonated. A nuclear weapon may be detonated in space, in the air at high or low altitude, on the surface, below the surface, or under water. Data in this appendix focuses on air bursts.

b. When detonated, a typical nuclear weapon will release its energy as blast, thermal radiation (including X-rays), nuclear radiation (alpha and beta particles, gamma rays, and neutrons), and electromagnetic pulse (EMP). (Figure C-1 depicts the relative proportions of

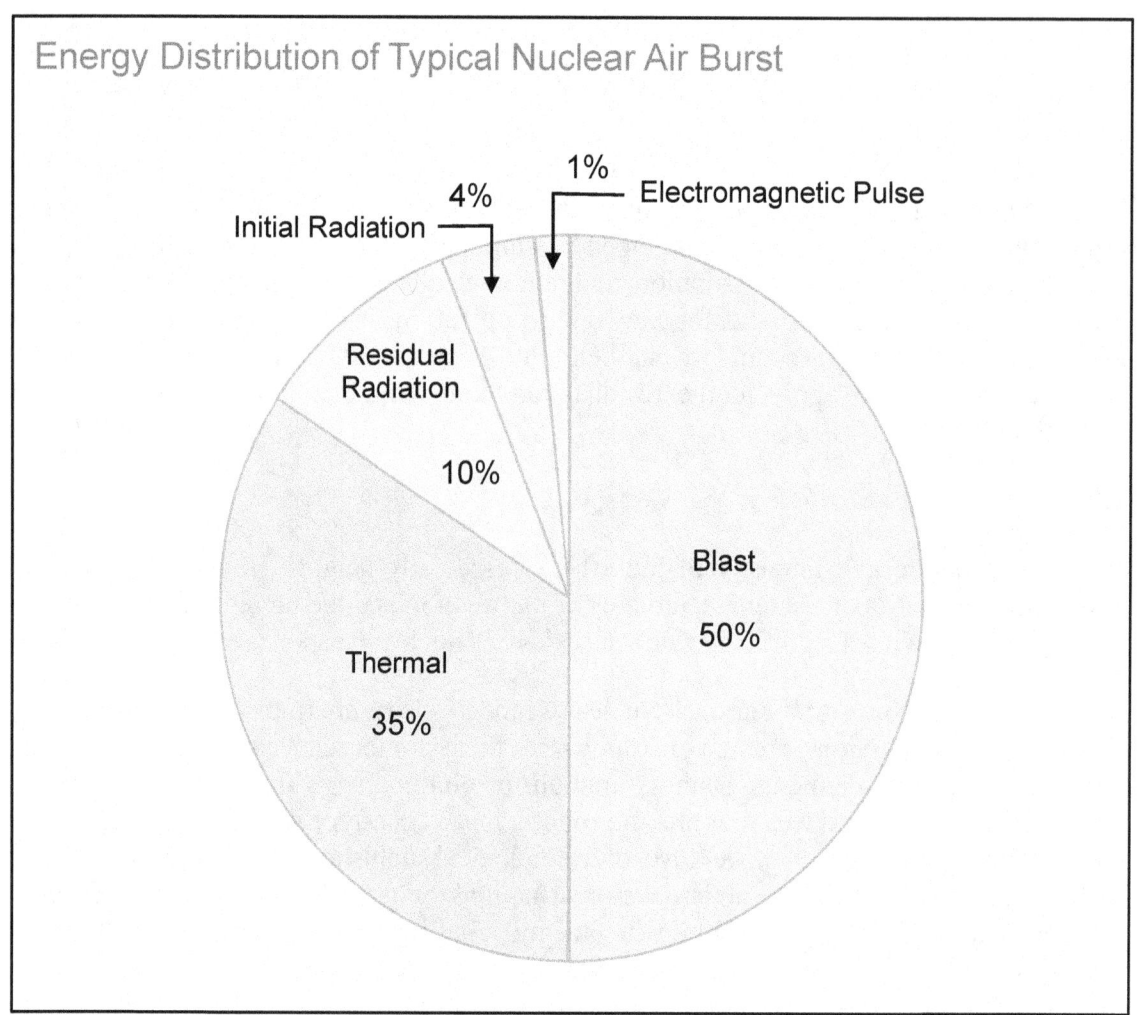

Figure C-1. Energy Distribution of Typical Nuclear Air Burst

the radiation products of an air burst nuclear explosion.) When the detonation occurs in the atmosphere, the primary radiation products interact with the surrounding air molecules and are absorbed by matter and scattered as they radiate from the point of detonation. The secondary radiation products, referred to as residual radiation or fallout, produce the preponderance of the radiation hazard and casualties beyond the immediate point of detonation. All of these interactions lead to the five significant effects of a nuclear weapon detonated in the air: blast, thermal radiation, ionizing radiation, fallout, and EMP.

For additional technical data, including nuclear weapon employment effects data, contact the United States Army Nuclear and Combating Weapons of Mass Destruction Field Operating Agency.

   c. **Blast.** A low-altitude nuclear air burst generates blast waves, high overpressures, and severe winds. These blast effects produce casualties and damage through crushing, bending, tumbling, and breaking. Many of the casualties will be injured from flying debris such as broken glass and rubble. Depending upon a weapon's yield and detonation location, the blast from a nuclear weapon is capable of destroying most of the infrastructure of a major city, including rendering roads impassable; disrupting water, sewer, gas, electrical, and phone lines; and destroying medical facilities. Commanders must anticipate these challenges when operating in a nuclear environment.

d. **Thermal Radiation.** The effect of the enormous amount of heat and light released by a nuclear detonation, in certain circumstances, may be more damaging than the blast. The thermal radiation from a multimegaton weapon can ignite wood, paper, rubber, plastics, and other materials many kilometers away from the detonation point. Because thermal radiation travels at the speed of light, flammable objects within the thermal range and line of sight of the blast will ignite immediately. Even a 10 kt weapon is capable of igniting flammable objects within several hundred meters of its detonation point. Additionally, thermal radiation will cause burns of various degrees to people in the line of sight of the explosion. Severe burn victims generally require intensive and sophisticated medical treatment, which may quickly overwhelm available medical support. Leaders must be aware of thermal radiation effects in order to operate in a nuclear environment.

e. **Ionizing Radiation.** Ionizing radiation produced from a nuclear detonation is generally split into two categories, initial radiation and residual radiation.

(1) Initial radiation (X-rays, gamma rays, and neutrons) is generally produced within the first minute of a detonation and is emitted directly from the nuclear reactions characteristic to the type of weapon employed.

(2) Residual radiation is produced from the environmental material, unfissioned weapon debris and radioactive fission products swept up into a debris cloud after the nuclear detonation occurs. This debris cloud will move with prevailing winds and will rain down to the ground as fallout depositing radioactivity over hundreds to thousands of kilometers around the detonation point. The resulting fallout produces residual radiation in the form of gamma, beta, and alpha particles and therefore becomes a significant hazard to personnel and materiel.

(3) Acute radiation doses from initial or residual radiation can cause biological harm, leading to severe illness or death. Additionally, intense ionizing radiation can damage objects, including optical, mechanical, and electronic components by altering their physical properties. Gamma rays and neutrons have a long range in the air and are highly penetrating. Consequently, even people inside of buildings and behind solid objects will receive some radiation dose.

f. **Fallout.** Fallout is the residual radiation product distributed into the atmosphere by a nuclear detonation. High-altitude bursts produce essentially no local fallout. For many weapon designs, low-altitude bursts in which the fireball does not touch the ground will very often produce little, in some cases negligible, amounts of fallout. All nuclear detonations close enough to the surface for the fireball to touch the ground produce very large amounts of radioactive debris that will be drawn up into the atmosphere and be deposited locally and dispersed downwind. Although fallout initially decays quickly, some areas could remain hazardous for years. Radiological surveys will be needed to identify and characterize such areas. Localized fallout may severely limit military operations within a contaminated area.

Civilian and military facilities and resources will most likely be overwhelmed by the requirements for fallout casualty decontamination, processing, and treatment. Additionally, decontamination, identification, and interment of remains are formidable challenges for commanders to overcome.

g. **EMP.** Nuclear generated EMP is a potential threat to all electronics and electrical systems. Its magnitude, duration, and waveshape are dependent upon the height of burst and weapon yield. EMP is generally described as high-altitude electromagnetic pulse (HEMP) and low-altitude electromagnetic pulse (LEMP).

(1) HEMP is a high-altitude detonation is of particular concern and can briefly cover many thousands of square kilometers of the earth's surface with an electromagnetic field capable of damaging or upsetting both mobile and fixed electrical systems.

(2) LEMP is generated by a low altitude or ground burst nuclear detonation with various nuclear weapons effects (already mentioned above). LEMP has a higher signal amplitude than HEMP but rapidly drops off in terms of strength as one moves away from the detonation point. This form of EMP is of primary concern to electrical based systems connected to long cables and will generate large electrical current pulses that can damage or destroy critical electronic components attached to the cables.

h. **Combined Effects.** Although each nuclear weapon effect is addressed separately, the planner should consider possible synergism of their combined effects on structures, equipment, and personnel. Structures may be burned, crushed, knocked down, and/or contaminated. Equipment may be disabled or destroyed by the combined effects of EMP, thermal blast, and ionizing radiation. Personnel may experience the effects of ionizing radiation in conjunction with conventional injury, and while each effect considered separately may not be sufficient to cause death, taken together, they could cause lethal damage.

4. Protective Actions

a. Protective actions taken before an attack are most effective for survivability of personnel and equipment. Mitigation can include, for example, wearing one or two layers of loose, light-colored clothing that can reduce burns; use of bunkers, reverse slopes, depressions, culverts, and caves; and dispersion. Education and training of leaders, staffs, and individuals on nuclear weapons effects and the principles of operations in CBRN environments can significantly enhance operational effectiveness in the event of nuclear attack.

For more details on individual and collective protective actions, see FM 3-11.4/MCWP 3-37.2/NTTP 3-11.27/AFTTP(I) 3-2.46, Multi-Service Tactics, Techniques, and Procedures for Nuclear, Biological, and Chemical (NBC) Protection.

b. Countermeasures such as potassium iodide may be used to protect the thyroid from radioactive iodine in the event of an accident or attack at a nuclear power plant, or other nuclear detonation, especially where volatile radionuclides, which contain significant amounts of iodine 131, are released into the environment. Radioiodine is a dangerous radionuclide because the body concentrates it in the thyroid gland. Potassium iodide cannot protect against other causes of radiation poisoning or provide protection against a radiological dispersal device (RDD) unless it contains radioactive iodine.

c. Commanders operating in radiological and nuclear environments must minimize and control the exposure of personnel to radiation. As described in Appendix D, "Radiological Hazard Considerations," an operational exposure guidance (OEG) must be established for all military operations.

See Appendix D, "Radiological Hazard Considerations," for further information on setting the OEG, radiation exposure status (RES) categories, military radiation exposure states, and risk criteria. FM 4-02.283/MCRP 4-11.1B/Navy Tactical Reference Publication (NTRP) 4-02.21/Air Force Manual (AFMAN) 44-161, *Multi-Service Tactics, Techniques, and Procedures for Treatment of Nuclear and Radiological Casualties.*

d. **EMP.** While a majority of military equipment is hardened against the effects of EMP, commercial-off-the-shelf items are not. Preventive measures include keeping cable runs as short as possible and not elevated, keeping enclosures shut, and ensuring any unused equipment is turned off and unplugged. When warnings are issued, penetration by EMP into equipment can be minimized by immediately shutting down electronic equipment (such as radios, computers, and generators) and disconnecting radio antennas and power cables.

Intentionally Blank

APPENDIX D
RADIOLOGICAL HAZARD CONSIDERATIONS

1. General

a. Radiation is ever-present and there is a background of natural radiation everywhere in our environment. It comes from space (i.e., cosmic rays) and from naturally occurring radioactive materials contained in the earth and in living things. The source of radiation may be natural, man-made, or technologically enhanced. Man-made sources are created by neutron bombardment and/or accelerators and include machine-generated radiation. Technologically enhanced sources are those that originate from natural radioactive materials found in the environment, but altered in a way as to concentrate or enhance radioactive material. Such sources can complicate detection and quantification of man-made radiation, and the interpretation of radiation measurements for identifying and marking a potential hazard area, making radiation risk management challenging.

b. Radiation hazards may arise from the presence of large amounts of natural radioactivity (high background), unintentional improper use of radioactive material, intentional use of radioactive material to kill or injure personnel, area denial purposes, or nuclear weapons detonation and fallout. Radiation threats differ from chemical and biological threats because radiation cannot be "neutralized" or "sterilized" and is not contagious. Further, exposure to radioactive material does not require direct contact.

c. Radiation should be differentiated from the radioactive material itself. Radiation is energy being carried away in the form of electromagnetic energy or as subatomic particles and so can act at some distance from the radioactive material itself. Radioactivity is a physical property of energetically unstable atoms, is measured by its characteristic half-life, and is unique for each radionuclide. Half-life describes the rate at which a specific radioactive material decays or changes from one nuclide to another nuclide that may in turn be radioactive or stable. Half-life can vary from a fraction of a second to many years, but once a material is stable, there is no longer an associated radiation hazard.

d. There are many variables that influence the human health impact of radiation exposure. A whole body exposure to penetrating radiation may result in immediate effects if delivered in large amounts over a short period of time, in cancer developed years later, or in no adverse medical conditions at all. The effects of radiation exposure are usually enhanced if there are other concurrent injuries, but there are medical countermeasures and treatments that can be employed to moderate the effects of the radiation exposure.

e. The Services are specifically responsible for establishing radiation safety policy and guidance for handling those military commodities, such as depleted uranium (DU) munitions, that contain radioactive materials and for participating in developing and enforcing exposure standards that protect personnel against external and internal exposure. In the operational area, the commander, in consultation with the staff, is responsible for managing risk for those within the command.

f. There are a variety of instruments that exist at various echelons designed to detect radiation. At the unit level, there are handheld devices (RADIAC [radiation, detection, indication, and computation]) equipment and dosimetry. Specialized units may have more advanced handheld devices, as well as laboratory grade equipment. Definitive quantitative measurements of air, water, and soils can be performed at service laboratories specializing in environmental radiation measurements. Background radiation must always be a consideration in the employment of radiation detection devices.

g. There are a number of methods to mitigate radiation hazards. The most straightforward and effective way is to avoid areas with radiation levels. If avoidance is not an option, then time, distance, and shielding should be used to limit exposure. Reduce the time of exposure, maximize the distance between the source and personnel, and utilize shielding material to reduce exposure. Individual protection and COLPRO can be used to preclude skin contamination and internal exposures via inhalation, ingestion, or injection. Decontamination methods can be used to limit exposure and potential cross-contamination. Finally, medical countermeasures can be used to limit internal uptake and medical treatments can lessen the effects of exposure.

h. A risk management tool to track and limit radiation exposures has been developed. RES is used to track unit exposure level, while the OEG is the commander's primary administrative control used to limit radiation exposure to personnel for a given mission.

2. The Radiological Threat

a. Introduction

(1) In addition to direct exposure to radiation and fallout from a nuclear detonation, there are many other potential sources of radiation. These sources can be broken down into four broad categories: natural, industrial, medical, and military commodities. The term toxic industrial radiological refers to any radiological material manufactured, used, transported, or stored by industrial, medical, or commercial processes. The mechanism of radiation production is by the decay of radioactive material by fission. The radiation is emitted in the form of neutrons, alpha particles, beta particles, gamma rays, or X-rays. Once radioactive material is introduced into the environment, it may be found in air, soil, and water, or as contamination on any object.

(2) Radioactive materials, to include fissionable materials, may be used by an aggressor in one or more of the following ways: as a nuclear device, an improvised nuclear device (IND), an RDD, and/or as a radiological exposure device (RED).

(3) The health effects of exposure to radiation and radioactive materials are immediate, deterministic effects, or latent, stochastic effects (effects that are delayed onset and have an increasing chance of occurrence with increasing dose). Many common radioactive materials also present a chemical toxicity hazard; this hazard may actually exceed that of the radiation. Deterministic effects are those in which the severity of the effect increases with dose above some threshold, below which there is no apparent effect, and only happens at relatively high doses. Large doses in a short time period may cause a

combination of deterministic effects termed acute radiation syndrome. The higher the dose, the faster these effects occur, and the more severe the syndrome will be. All doses of radiation also have the potential to cause an increase in an individual's risk of cancer. Since the probability of the effect (cancer risk) increases with dose, it is termed nondeterministic. Note the severity of nondeterministic effects is unaffected by increasing dose (i.e., an individual either has cancer or does not, and there is no threshold). Occupational radiation safety programs and regulations are designed to preclude deterministic effects and limit nondeterministic effects to an acceptable level. Figure D-1 summarizes the overall effects of radiation exposure as a function of dose for healthy, young adults with no other injuries. The threshold for deterministic effects will be lower for personnel with combined injuries. Medical intervention can limit some effects and increase survivability.

b. **Sources of Radiation**

Effects of Radiation Exposure

Acute Dose centi-Gray (cGy) Free-in-Air	Threshold Effects Within 1 Day (See Notes 1, 2)	Probability of Death Within 30 Days	Probability of Nausea/ Vomiting Within 6 Hours	Percent Expected to Require Hospitalizations	Probability of Death from Excess Cancer (40 Years After Exposure) (See Note 3)
35	None expected	< 1%	< 1%	< 1%	< 1%
75	Mild – Nausea – Vomiting – Headache	< 1%	< 10%	< 1%	1-2%
125	• Lymphocyte count drop • Fever	< 1%	< 25%	< 10%	2-4%
410	• Moderate vomiting • Diarrhea • Fatigue	≥ 50%	75%	100%	10-15%
1000	Performance degraded	≥ 99%	100%	100%	n/a
3000	Combat ineffective	100%	100%	100%	n/a
8000	• Disorientation • Death				

rad = radiation absorbed dose

1 rad = 1 cGy

100 rad = 1 Gray

NOTES:

1. The probability of death is without medical treatment and for healthy adults.

2. Burns and/or trauma in combination with radiation injury increases mortality. Personnel with such injuries combined with radiation doses exceeding 100 cGy will likely require prompt medical evaluation. Personnel with combined injuries with doses in excess of 600 cGy are unlikely to survive regardless of medical intervention.

3. US citizens have approximately 41% chance of getting cancer over lifetime, averaging between 37% and 41% based upon race and ethnicity.

Figure D-1. Effects of Radiation Exposure

(1) Nuclear detonation and fallout

(2) Natural sources of radiation include those of both terrestrial and cosmic origin. Terrestrial radionuclides found in the Earth's crust include uranium and thorium decay chains and K-40 [potassium-40], among others. The Earth is exposed to cosmic radiation, which gives rise to atmospheric P-32 [phosphorus-32], C-14 [carbon-14], H-3 [tritium], among others. These are the main contributors to background radiation, along with worldwide fallout from above ground nuclear weapons testing.

(3) Industrial sources of radiation include cargo inspection systems, industrial X-ray machines, accelerators, sterilizers for food and medical instruments, well hole loggers, and moisture density gauges. A few of the nuclides most commonly used for these applications are Co-60 [cobalt-60], Cs-137 [cesium-137], and Ir-192 [iridium-192]. Nuclear weapons production and the nuclear fuel cycle, including mining and milling, fuel production, reactor operations, reprocessing and waste, also falls in this category. There are many nuclides associated with these processes, but a few of the more well-known, long-lived radionuclides are uranium (U-234, U-235, and U-238), DU (primarily U-238), plutonium (Pu-238, Pu-239, and Pu-240), Ra-226 [radium-226], Rn-222 [radon-222], Cs-137, I-131 [iodine-131], and Sr-90 [strontium-90].

(4) Medical sources of radiation again include machine-generated radiation from medical accelerators, X-ray, and computed tomography (CT) machines. Among the radionuclides commonly used in medicine are H-3 and C-14 as tracers; Mo-99 [molybdenum-99]/Tc-99m [technetium-99m], Xe-133 [xenon-133], I-131, Ir-192, Co-60, F-18 [fluorine-18], and Tl-201 [thallium-201] for diagnosis and treatment of disease and injury.

(5) Military commodities encompass all radioactive materials used in military equipment. There are many radionuclides to be found on or in military equipment. The most common use is as a luminous agent (to make things glow in the dark). Generally, either Ra-226 or H-3 is used for this application. Some of the other more commonly encountered materials are Ni-63 [nickel-63], Am-241 [americium-241], DU, Pm-147 [promethium-147], Th-232 [thorium-232], Cs-137, and Co-60.

c. **Mechanisms of Radiation Production**

(1) The most commonly encountered means of radiation production is machine generation. In medicine, exposure to radiation occurs during X-ray, CT, and particle-accelerator-related treatments. Machine-generated radiation is also used in industrial X-ray machines and in inspection devices for baggage, cargo, and most recently, passengers. In research, electron microscopes and X-ray diffraction equipment produce radiation. Machine-generated radiation equipment requires electrical power to produce radiation and is only hazardous when powered and activated, although there may be residual radioactive activation products formed in building materials in the vicinity of high-energy accelerators.

(2) Radioactive material produces radiation by the physical process of nuclear decay. Nuclear decay occurs when an energetically unstable nuclei (parent nuclide) emits energy or radiation as it becomes a more stable (progeny) nuclide that may be either

radioactive or stable. The decay process is governed by a physical constant unique to that particular parent nuclide called half-life. An example is the isotope of uranium with an atomic mass of 238 (U-238): U-238 decays into thorium 234 (Th-234) via alpha decay with a half-life of 4.5 billion years. The long half-life of U-238 is the reason it is found in the Earth's crust. U-238 has been in the Earth's crust since the formation of the Earth, about one of its half-lives ago. Radioactive material remains a hazard until the material decays into an inconsequential quantity (the rule of thumb is seven half-lives of the nuclide), although there may be radioactive progeny that also need to be considered during the risk management process. Since decay is a physical process at an atomic scale, it cannot be altered via inactivation or decomposition like chemical and biological hazards can. Further, radioactivity can be a hazard at some distance from the source radioactive material, due to penetrating radiation. Decontamination can physically remove exterior radioactive particles, but they remain a hazard in the waste stream. Radioactive material, once internalized, can remain in the bodies of exposed personnel for the lifetime of the individual. PPE (Joint Service Lightweight Integrated Suit Technology and Joint Protective Aircrew Ensemble and protective mask) can prevent particulate internal exposure. It must be noted, however, that PPE does not protect against radiation. PPE will keep alpha and beta particles from touching an individual; a mask will protect from inhalation of radioactive particles. Neither of these offers protection from gamma or X-ray radiation. Protection is discussed in further detail in following sections.

(3) Radiation may be produced by fission of certain radionuclides, such as U-235 and Pu-239, which are used to make nuclear fuel and nuclear weapons. Fission involves the splitting of atoms into two fission fragments, and the emission of radiation in the form of one or more neutrons and gamma rays. Spontaneous fission can occur, but fission is more likely initiated by a neutron being absorbed within the parent nuclide. If one or more neutrons are produced within a quantity of fissionable material, a chain reaction occurs, potentially leading to a nuclear detonation, releasing large amounts of energy. The amount of material in a specific configuration required to generate a chain reaction is called the critical mass. Fissionable nuclides can undergo nuclear decay, typically via alpha decay, with relatively long half-lives. In subcritical masses, fissionable material is fairly inert, although two initially subcritical masses, when brought together, can emit lethal amounts of radiation and possibly detonate. Separation of subcritical masses is imperative.

d. **Types of Radiation**

(1) Neutrons originate in the nucleus of an atom, have no charge and a substantial mass (~1 atomic mass unit [amu]). They are penetrating (may act at long distances) and have variable health effects depending upon their energy. They are difficult to detect and require specialized equipment not commonly found in the field. Low Z (low atomic number) materials make good neutron shielding, especially hydrogenous materials such as plastic or water.

(2) Alpha particles are large (~4 amu) charged (+2) helium nuclei. They are produced by unstable nuclei with excess energy and an excess of protons (alpha decay reduces the proton/neutron ratio). Because of their relatively large size and charge, they have a very short range (a few centimeters in air, a few microns in tissue) and deposit a great

amount of energy in a relatively short path length. Alpha particles are difficult to detect in the field due to their short range and limited ability to penetrate into the volume of a detector. Alpha particles are easily shielded by a piece of paper or human skin. Therefore, health effects of alpha exposure occur only when the particles are inhaled, ingested, or enter the body through a cut in the skin. More serious would be a material that is radioactive (alpha emitter) that is ingested into the body. The alpha particles emitted inside the body, for example in bone marrow, can be exceedingly dangerous.

(3) Beta particles are electrons or positrons that are ejected from the nucleus of an unstable atom. They have a mass of about 0.0005 amu and a charge of −1 and +1 respectively. They deposit much less energy per unit path length than an alpha particle, and so have substantial range (meters in air, millimeters in tissue). Typically, they are relatively easy to detect with commonly fielded handheld radiation detection equipment. There are notable exceptions to this general rule: both carbon-14 and tritium are difficult to detect due to the very low energy of the beta particle; illustrating that just because you do not detect any radiation, does not mean there is not any present. Note that skin contamination with beta emitters can cause burns. Shielding is normally accomplished with low Z (i.e., low atomic number) materials such as plexiglass and aluminum.

(4) Gamma and X-rays are essentially the same, except for their point of origin. Gamma rays originate in the nucleus of the atom, while X-rays originate in the electron cloud of the atom. Their energy spectra overlap, but X-rays are generally lower in energy than gamma rays. Both gamma and X-rays are electromagnetic energy with no mass and no charge and are very penetrating. They are easy to detect with handheld field detection systems. Most radionuclides will have some relatively abundant gamma and/or X-ray associated with their decay, even if they have another primary mode of decay, allowing them to be detected with typical handheld instrumentation. Dense materials such as steel and lead are typically used as shielding for gamma and X-rays.

e. **Employment.** The previous discussion has outlined radiological sources that are in legitimate use throughout the world, but there are means to use these sources as weapons. In addition to attacking and destroying facilities where radioactive material is used and/or stored (e.g., nuclear reactors), leading to distribution of radioactive material in the environment, radiological material can be offensively employed in nuclear weapons, INDs, REDs, and RDDs. The efficacy of radiological weapons, other than nuclear weapons, at inflicting casualties, is not high. They are, however, well suited to creating fear and as area denial weapons.

(1) A relatively small number of countries has nuclear weapons capability, because they are technically difficult and expensive to produce. Other than open war with another nuclear capable country, the probability of nuclear explosion is low. Nuclear devices produced by nuclear capable countries are difficult to detonate without proper equipment and security codes. This makes them unlikely candidates for use on the battlefield in less than total war with a nuclear capable enemy. If used at the optimum height of burst, it would generate prompt radiation, EMP causing extensive damage to electronic equipment, conventional damage, and injury, but likely very little fallout.

(2) A non-state actor could produce an IND from illegally obtained fissionable material, such as enriched uranium and plutonium. There would be significant technical problems that would have to be solved in order to produce the IND, but with the right expertise, it may be possible. An IND would likely be a low-yield nuclear device detonated on the ground delivering prompt radiation exposure and conventional damage and injury, as well as significant fallout.

(3) An RED is simply a penetrating radiation source (gamma and/or neutron) that is placed or buried where people will become exposed to the radiation emitted. An RED is relatively easily employed, but obtaining the material might be difficult. If a relatively large source of penetrating radiation could be obtained, it could be emplaced in a public location, such as a park or public building, in such a way as to maximize the probability and time of exposure to those nearby. If the source were big enough and the time of exposure long enough, exposure could lead to acute effects such as nausea, diarrhea, and erythema (reddening of the skin), leading to clinical illness and death.

(4) An RDD is a device, other than a nuclear explosive device, designed to disseminate radioactive material in order to cause destruction, damage, or injury. This is done by using a conventional explosive bundled with radioactive material. The explosive itself would likely cause most of the direct damage and injury, but the radioactive contamination may deny use of the area and complicate incident management and health services support. Mitigation of the effects of the contamination would consume significant resources. Additionally, it may not be routine for IED response to utilize radiation detection equipment to confirm the presence of radioactive material, delaying recognition of the RDD event and further complicating effective response and risk management. The radiation itself may not pose an immediate health threat, but contamination control measures and protective measures (IPE, PPE) should be implemented to reduce risk of future health implications. (See Figure D-1.)

3. Radiological Threat Management

a. **Responsibilities.** The commander is responsible for managing risk on behalf of all personnel under the commander's authority. It is DOD policy to reduce exposure to ionizing radiation associated with DOD operations to a level as low as reasonably achievable (ALARA) consistent with operational risk management. Complying with the principle of ALARA must be done in the context of managing risk from all sources. Commanders must balance risk management with the requirement of completing the military mission.

(1) **Operational Commanders**

(a) Set the OEG.

(b) Establish guidance for the use of radioprotectants.

(c) Review radiological risk throughout mission; revise guidance if necessary.

(2) **Staffs**

(a) Conduct radiological risk management.

(b) Provide risk estimate and mitigation recommendations to the commander.

(c) Implement medical surveillance program.

(d) Recommend guidance for the use of radiotherapeutics.

(e) Collect/archive cumulative dose information.

(f) Prepare radiological risk updates as mission progresses; recommend additional mitigation measures and/or revised guidance if circumstances dictate.

b. **Detection and Measurement**

(1) **Handheld Radiation Detection Equipment**

(a) Only in very peculiar circumstances will an individual be able to sense radiation without the aid of some detection device, and there are no universal radiation detection systems that are appropriate for every type of radiation detection scenario. Each system has its advantages and disadvantages. The selection of the appropriate radiation detection system is dependent upon many variables, including the type of radiation (alpha, beta, gamma, neutron) that is of interest, the environmental media or circumstances (air, water, soil, surface, volume, or ambient), the type of measurement that is needed (e.g., removable contamination, cumulative dose, dose rate, exposure, exposure rate, counts per minute, etc.), and the need to determine radionuclide identity. Detection equipment generally provides indication well before radiation levels present a health hazard.

Note that a negative response on a given piece of radiation detection equipment does not necessarily indicate radiation and/or radioactive material are not present; it indicates that particular piece of equipment is unable to detect any radiation.

(b) The most commonly available and most useful radiation detection instruments are capable of measuring ambient and surface dose and dose rate from gamma and beta emitting nuclides. CBRN specialists, bioenvironmental engineers, industrial hygiene specialists, and health physicists are able to detect and measure gamma rays, and alpha and beta particles using specialized probes. Available through a radiation safety officer, there may be specialized instruments in theater that can provide nuclide identification capability for gamma-emitting nuclides. Some dosimeters are neutron sensitive.

(2) **Personnel Radiation Dosimetry.** Field dosimetry systems are fielded to those units that have a requirement to track the radiation dose of their personnel. A difference should be noted between real-time reading dosimeters (such as an electronic personal dosimeter or a color-changing dosimeter) and those that require separate equipment and extra time to read. An unforeseen requirement for dosimetry may arise that necessitates establishing a dosimetry program or augmenting the program already in place. In this eventuality, the following Service agencies can be contacted for guidance and support:

(a) US Army Dosimetry Center
ATTN: AMSAM-TMD-SD, Building 5417
Redstone Arsenal, AL 35898-5000
Phone: 256-876-1786
Fax: 256-876-3816

(b) US Air Force Radiation Dosimetry Laboratory
2510 5th Street, Area B, Building 0840
Wright-Patterson Air Force Base, OH 45433-7212
Phone: 937-938-3358
Fax: 937-904-6322
E-mail: usafsam.oeworkflow@wpafb.af.mil

(c) Naval Dosimetry Center
Walter Reed National Military Medical Center
8901 Wisconsin Avenue
Bethesda, MD 20889-5614
Phone: 301-295-5410
Fax: 301-295-5981

(3) Laboratory Grade Capabilities. Laboratory capability in a field environment is likely to be very limited or nonexistent. This level of measurement is usually reserved for environmental samples that are taken in the field and then sent to a laboratory outside the theater of operations. This capability can be accessed through the following Service contacts:

(a) US Army Institute of Public Health Laboratory Sciences Portfolio
USAPHC
ATTN: MCHB-TS-L
5158 Blackhawk Road
Aberdeen Proving Ground, MD 21010-5403
Phone: 410-436-3639
DSN: 584-3639

(b) US Air Force School of Aerospace Medicine
2510 5th Street, Building 840
Wright-Patterson Air Force Base, OH 45433-7913
Phone: 937-938-2716
DSN: 798-2716

(c) Environmental, Safety, and Occupational Health (ESOH) Service Center
esoh.service.center@wpafb.af.mil
Toll Free: 1-888-232-ESOH (3764)
Phone: 937-938-3764
DSN: 798-3764
Fax: 937-656-8637

Field radiation detection, measurement, and survey techniques are detailed in ATP 3-11.37/ MCWP 3-37.4/NTTP 3-11.29/AFTTP 3-2.44, Multi-Service Tactics, Techniques, and Procedures for Chemical, Biological and Nuclear Reconnaissance and Surveillance.

   c. **Radiological Contamination Mitigation**

     (1) **Principles of Radiation Protection**

       (a) If radiation is encountered and the mission requires potential exposure, the three principles of radiation protection, time, distance, and shielding, can be applied to minimize exposures. Minimizing time of exposure in an elevated radiation environment minimizes dose. Mission permitting, practice tasks that will have to be performed in a radiological environment before execution so that they can be performed more quickly. Rotate personnel in and out of the radiological environment so that no single individual is excessively exposed. Sometimes forgoing the use of IPE that might slow operations can shorten time of exposure and minimize dose.

       (b) Distance has an inverse square relationship to radiation exposure or dose, meaning that if the distance from the source is increased by a factor of X, the dose is decreased by a factor of X^2, e.g., double the distance, quarter the dose. Maximizing personnel distance from the source will minimize dose. If only one person is needed to perform a mission in close proximity to a source, send only one. Other supporting staff can be located a greater distance away, minimizing dose. Individuals should also be cognizant of their geometry in relationship to the source so that they can position themselves at the maximum distance from the source, consistent with mission accomplishment. If the source is contamination on the ground and is fairly uniformly distributed, standing or sitting some distance above the ground in a vehicle or elevated platform will also minimize dose, as well as act as a shield.

       (c) Shielding is simply placing material between personnel and a source. The reduction of the dose depends on the type of radiation being emitted, the shielding material, as well as its density and thickness. Thicker is always better, but may be limited by weight and availability. Lead and other dense materials work well for gamma and X-ray emitters. Lower density means greater thickness is required for the same shielding value. Lower density material such as plexiglass or aluminum should be used to shield against beta emitters. Beta interaction with high-density materials like lead can lead to significant X-ray production, possibly increasing dose. Neutrons can be shielded with materials that have a lot of hydrogen atoms, like plastics and water. Generally, it is not necessary to shield for alpha particles. Concrete, earth, and sand bags can work well as field expedient shielding material for all sources. In addition, vehicles will provide shielding, with armored vehicles generally providing more shielding than light vehicles. Note that IPE does not provide shielding for the most part, but it can limit contamination and internal uptake of radioactive material, thereby limiting dose.

     (2) **Avoidance.** Avoiding sources of radiation is obviously the most effective means of limiting radiation risk, but may increase other risks, e.g., choosing to go around a contaminated area might subject a unit to the physical risk of a mine field or increased

likelihood of ambush. Based on mission requirements, the use of a unmanned ground vehicle will prevent the unnecessary exposure of personnel to sources of radiation.

Avoidance is discussed in detail in FM 3-11.3/MCRP 3-37.2A/NTTP 3-11.25/AFTTP(I) 3-2.56, Multi-Service Tactics, Techniques, and Procedures for Chemical, Biological, Radiological, and Nuclear Contamination Avoidance.

(3) **Personal Protection and COLPRO.** Utilization of IPE and COLPRO can control contamination and limit internalization of radioactive material, which is particularly important for alpha emitters. Some COLPRO systems may also have some shielding value, although this is not the case with IPE.

CBRN protection is discussed in detail in FM 3-11.4/MCWP 3-37.2/NTTP 3-11.27/AFTTP(I) 3-2.46, Multi-Service Tactics, Techniques, and Procedures for Nuclear, Biological, and Chemical (NBC) Protection.

(4) **Decontamination.** Decontamination is the process of making any person, object, or area safe by absorbing, destroying, neutralizing, making harmless, or removing chemical or biological agents, or by removing radioactive material clinging to or around it. Radioactive contamination is generally associated with particulates, although there are some materials that will be found as gasses or vapors. No special decontamination solution is required for radioactive material, since the hazard cannot be reduced by chemical or physical destruction. Waste material generated as a result of decontamination should be controlled and disposed of in accordance with appropriate command TTP and/or HN disposal procedures.

Decontamination is discussed in detail in FM 3-11.5/MCWP 3-37.3/NTTP 3-11.26/AFTTP(I) 3-2.60, Multi-Service Tactics, Techniques, and Procedures for Chemical, Biological, Radiological, and Nuclear Decontamination.

(5) **Medical Countermeasures and Treatment.** There are pretreatment drugs that can be given prior to exposure to limit the effects of radiation exposure. Anti-emetics will keep personnel from vomiting following radiation exposure. Potassium iodide can limit the uptake of radio-iodine, a fission product found in fallout from a nuclear detonation or reactor accident. There are general pre-treatments currently under development and potentially available in the future that can act to lessen the biological damage caused by the radiation. Post-exposure, there are a number of drugs that can be given to biologically remove radioactive material from the body. EDTA [ethylenediaminetetraacetic acid] and DTPA [diethylenetriaminepentaacetic acid] are metal scavengers that can be used, but only under medical monitoring since they can be poisonous if the dose is not carefully controlled. Prussian blue can be administered to treat internal exposure to Cs-137, another common fission fragment.

Medical countermeasures and treatment are discussed in detail in FM 4-02.283/MCRP 4-11.1B/NTRP 4-02.21/AFMAN 44-161(I), Treatment of Nuclear and Radiological Casualties.

d. **Risk Management**

The Food and Drug Administration has determined that 500 milligram Prussian blue generic capsules, when manufactured under the conditions of an approved new drug application, can be found safe and effective for the treatment of known or suspected internal contamination with radioactive cesium, radioactive thallium, or nonradioactive thallium. "Prussian blue" is the generic name of the blue-colored capsules. Different brand names of the Prussian blue generic capsules are available. The term "Prussian blue" refers to a variety of bluish pigment.

Prussian blue works using a mechanism known as ion exchange. Cesium or thallium that have been absorbed into the body are removed by the liver and passed into the intestine and are then re-absorbed into the body (enterohepatic circulation refers to the circulation system between the liver and the intestine). Prussian blue works by trapping thallium and cesium in the intestine, so that they can be passed out of the body in the stool rather than be re-absorbed. If persons are exposed to radioactive cesium, radioactive thallium, or nonradioactive thallium, taking Prussian blue may reduce the risk of death and major illness from radiation or poisoning.

Various Sources

(1) The commander's decision to expose personnel to ionizing radiation should be balanced with mission requirements and all other risks. In combat, it may be necessary to exceed safe levels of radiation exposure due to mission requirements or as a consequence of enemy action. The risk management process is to identify hazards, characterize the risks to the greatest extent possible, and apply mitigation measures to try to eliminate or minimize the risks. The goal is to achieve the lowest possible overall risk consistent with mission accomplishment.

(2) The staff planner should be aware that risk mitigation measures applied to reduce risk associated with one hazard may increase risk to another hazard. As part of the risk management process, applying radiation safety mitigation measures should act in concert with other risk mitigation measures to minimize the overall risk. The highest risk of significant casualties will usually occur from the conventional weapons threat. Increasing conventional risk to achieve the goal of ALARA may result in an increased total risk with higher probability of mission failure.

(3) Complete risk management requires the following:

(a) Information. The staff should work to collect the best available information on all the identified hazards. The risk assessment begins with accurate information on the nature of all hazards present in the operational area, to include intelligence assessments, measurements, visual observations, and modeling.

(b) Justification. During operational decision making, commanders should consider immediate, operationally significant health effects as well as long-term consequences of radiation exposure, e.g., cancer, in addition to all other health risks. The importance of the mission should drive acceptability of risk.

(c) Optimization. After a risk has been justified, the commander should optimize the plan to minimize the potential effects of all risks that are involved, in the context of the mission. The operational implications of risk mitigation measures should be carefully considered. Optimization balances potential reduction in operational effectiveness inherent in instituting some risk mitigation measures with the potential return in the reduction of risk. For example, use of IPE slows operations but provides protection against internalization of radioactive materials, limiting internal dose; effectiveness of the tradeoff in reducing overall risk should be evaluated before a given risk mitigation measure is adopted.

(4) The dose contributed by ingestion or inhalation of radioactive material (known as internal dose) by partial body irradiations from gamma rays and by skin irradiations from beta particles is difficult to accurately assess in the field. However, such individual doses can be estimated by appropriately trained staff for operational purposes. Depending upon the type of radioactive material and its dispersed form, the combined internal and external dose equivalent may be much larger than the external exposure recorded on a dosimeter. Consequently, respiratory and skin protection must be considered whenever the hazard analysis establishes a potential risk in which the internal exposure, or skin exposure, will cause the commander's OEG to be exceeded. Implementation of respiratory and skin protection controls will be subject to common sense tests of being reasonably achievable and practical for the situation.

4. Operational Radiological Risk Management Tools

a. RES

(1) RES provides a convenient method to track dose and associated operational impact of exposure. Since RES is directly related to effects of tactical interest, it can be used for estimating the effectiveness of units (or, in exceptional cases, of individuals) and is considered during operational planning to select units or individuals with appropriate capabilities or skills to ensure mission accomplishment that results in the lowest RES after the mission is completed.

(2) Tracking RES includes keeping and maintaining RES records. RES is an estimate, indicated by the categorization symbols RES-0 through RES-3 (see Figure D-2), which may be applied to a unit, subunit, or exceptionally, to an individual. It is based on total cumulative dose received from exposure to penetrating radiation. The total cumulative dose is most accurately determined by using a dosimeter (see paragraph 3.b.(2), "Personnel Radiation Dosimetry"). If a dosimeter is not used, then the dose can be estimated based on radiation monitoring data and total exposure time. Special advisors (see paragraph 6, "Service Resources") should be consulted for acceptable, alternative methods of assessing these exposures. All individuals of the unit or subunit are assigned the same RES based on the determined dose. If personnel are reassigned, the unit RES is determined by the average dose of the individuals assigned. All personnel who have received radiation exposure during operations should be evaluated by medical personnel, and appropriate entries documented in their individual medical record in accordance with multi-Service TTP and NATO standardization agreement (STANAG) 2473, *Commander's Guide to Radiation Exposures in Non-Article 5 Crisis Response Operations*. Figure D-2 defines the RES categories as a

Radiation Exposure Status Categories

Total Cumulative Dose (See Notes 1 & 2)	Radiation Exposure Status (RES) Category	Recommended Actions (Continue Actions from the Previous RES Categories as RES Increases)
0 – 0.05 cGy	RES-0	• Routine monitoring for early warning of hazard
0.05 – 0.5 cGy	RES-1A	• Record individual/unit dose readings • Initiate specific mission protocols or goals
0.5 – 5 cGy	RES-1B	• Initiate radiation survey and continue monitoring
5 – 10 cGy	RES-1C	• Update survey and continue monitoring • Continue dose control measures • Execute PRIORITY tasks only (see note 3)
10 – 25 cGy	RES-1D	• Execute CRITICAL tasks only (see note 4) • Medical evaluation recommended upon normally scheduled return to home station
25 – 75 cGy (see note 5)	RES-1E	• Monitor for acute radiation syndrome symptoms
75 – 125 cGy (see note 5)	RES-2	• Any further exposure exceeds moderate operational risk
> 125 cGy (see note 5)	RES-3	• All further exposure will exceed the emergency operational risk

1 rad = 1 radiation absorbed dose = 1 centi-Gray (cGy)

NOTES:

1. Radiation measurement in either centisievert (cSv) or millisievert (mSv) is preferred in all cases. However, due to the fact that the military may only have the capability to measure centi-gray (cGy) or milligray (mGy), the radiation guidance tables are presented in units of cGy for convenience. For whole body gamma irradiation, 10 mGy = 1 cGy = 1 cSv = 10 mSv.

2. All doses should be kept as low as reasonably achievable. This will reduce individual soldier risk as well as retain maximum operational flexibility for future employment of exposed soldiers.

3. Examples of priority tasks are those that contain the hazard, avert danger to persons, or allow the mission to continue without major revisions in the operational plan.

4. Examples of critical tasks are those that save lives or allow continued support that is deemed essential by the operational commander to conduct the mission.

5. Although an upper bound for RES 1E is provided in the table, it is conceivable that doses to personnel could exceed this amount. A low incidence of acute radiation sickness can be expected as whole body doses start to exceed 75 cGy. Personnel exceeding the RES 1E limit should be considered for medical evaluation and evacuation upon any signs or symptoms related to acute radiation sickness (e.g., nausea, vomiting, anorexia, fatigue).

Figure D-2. Radiation Exposure Status Categories

function of dose received by the unit and describes the precautions required for units in each of the RES categories. The Service dosimetry centers are the primary location for all exposure and dose information processing. Each Service maintains a repository of individual dose information. In some cases, dosimetry results may be forwarded from the individual Service dosimetry centers to Defense Occupational and Environmental Health Readiness System surveillance data portal for analysis and archiving at https://doehrswww.apgea.army.mil/doehrsdr/.

b. **Assessing Radiation Hazards**

(1) Determining if the radiological hazards can be controlled depends on whether they are sufficiently characterized and appropriate controls are in place or can be put in place, and sufficient resources exist to protect personnel to a level of risk comparable to occupational standards. Under such conditions commanders should apply the same standards of ionizing radiation protection as would apply to any routine practice involving ionizing radiation exposure and radioactive material as specified in DODI 6055.08, *Occupational Ionizing Radiation Protection Program.* Commanders may require that dose limits specified in DODI 6055.08 be exceeded in emergency situations and during combat or wartime military operations.

(2) A sufficiently characterized radiological hazard will normally include an evaluation of the environment by a radiation SME such as a health physicist or radiation specialist. Characterization normally includes identifying the radionuclide(s) (or ionizing radiation type, radiation energy, and half-life of the source), quantifying the dose rate, and determining how the dose rate will change over time. Commanders should consult with available expertise and use available resources to characterize the environment to the best of their ability. Reachback and staff augmentation is available from several sources within each Service and DTRA, Joint Task Force–Civil Support, and the Armed Forces Radiobiology Research Institute.

(3) In contrast, environments are uncontrolled when they are uncharacterized, and/or limited resources exist to reduce personnel exposure to ionizing radiation. Under such circumstances, commanders should apply operational risk management to protect personnel to the greatest extent possible. Requirements under these conditions include ensuring exposures are both justified and ALARA, as well as applying OEG instead of dose limits.

c. **Determine the Radiological Risk**

(1) In order to assess the risk in a radiological environment, estimate the potential dose and dose rate from radiological sources that may be encountered during the mission. This will determine the severity of the radiological threat. Next, determine the likelihood of encountering this radiological threat. This will determine the probability of exposure. Figures D-3 and D-4 provide severity and probability descriptions.

(2) Once the severity and the probability of the hazard are determined, Figure D-5 correlates the two to determine the level of risk associated with the hazard.

d. **Setting an OEG**

(1) The OEG is set for each platoon or equivalent unit and for each mission. The OEG should be based on the importance of the mission and the acceptable tolerance to ionizing radiation effects in comparison to other risks associated with the mission. During the risk management process, an approach is begun by selecting a conservatively low OEG. As an example, use Figure D-6 to determine OEG and assess the impact to the mission. If there is no foreseeable impact on the mission, then the low OEG should be appropriate. If

Severity of Radiological Threat

Level of Severity	Mission Impact	Associated Potential Dose and Dose Rate
Catastrophic	• Expected loss of ability to accomplish mission	• Total dose > 450 centi-Grays • Encounter source/environment with dose rate > 200 centi-Grays per hour
Critical	• Expected significant degradation of mission capabilities in terms of the required mission standard • Inability to accomplish all parts of the mission • Inability to accomplish the mission to standard if hazards occur during the mission	• Total dose > 200 centi-Grays • Encounter source/environment with dose rate > 10 centi-Grays per hour
Marginal	• Expected degraded mission capabilities in terms of the required mission standard; mission capability will be reduced if hazards occur during the mission	• Total dose > 75 centi-Grays • Encounter source/environment with dose rate > 0.5 centi-Grays per hour
Negligible	• Expected effect will have little or no impact on accomplishing the mission	• Total dose > 25 centi-Grays • Encounter source/environment with dose rate > 0.01 centi-Grays per hour

1 rad = 1 centi-Gray

Figure D-3. Severity of Radiological Threat

not, raise the guidance to a less conservative (i.e., higher) OEG and repeat the process. Note that the risks should be monitored and reassessed as needed throughout the mission, allowing the OEG to be modified as necessary to keep risks as low as practical.

(2) The recommended levels for the exposure guidance given in Figure D-6 are low enough that the primary risk is limited to an increased risk of long-term health effects except for a critical mission with an extremely high acceptable risk. This table is intended to guide commanders and their staffs in determining an appropriate OEG.

(3) **Critical** missions are those missions that are essential to the overall success of a higher headquarters' operation, emergency lifesaving missions, or the equivalent.

(4) **Priority** missions are those missions that avert danger to persons, prevent damage from spreading, or support the organization's mission-essential task list.

(5) **Routine** missions are all other missions that are not designated as priority or critical missions.

Probability of Radiological Threat

Probability of Event	Impact on Personnel
Frequent – 1 in 500	• Expected to occur several times or continuously over the duration of a specific mission
Likely – 1 in 1,000	• Expected to occur during a specific mission or at a high rate but intermittently
Occasional – 1 in 10,000	• May occur as often as not during a specific mission • Occurs sporadically
Seldom – 1 in 100,000	• Not expected to occur during a mission • Occurs rarely as isolated incidents
Unlikely	• Occurrence not impossible but can assume will not occur during a mission • Occurs very rarely

Figure D-4. Probability of Radiological Threat

(6) In all cases, if following the OEG introduces additional risks and/or hazards otherwise avoidable, a reassessment of the OEG is warranted. It is not reasonable to set the OEG so low that it introduces other more severe and/or unnecessary risks. For example, if the OEG is set so that a route is not usable because of the possibility of exceeding the OEG, and other routes introduce the potential for unnecessary adversary engagement or other significant danger, then reassess the risks and the importance of the mission, consider additional dose reduction mitigation measures, and/or increase the OEG.

e. Commanders should establish an OEG for the following situations:

(1) All missions with the potential for ionizing radiation exposure.

(2) Units conducting radiological decontamination for personnel or equipment.

(3) Units conducting immediate or operational decontamination.

(a) Unlike chemical or biological agents, radiation will not be neutralized by decontamination. Decontamination will only move the hazard from one surface (bodies, vehicles, etc.) to another (the containment). Removed contaminated clothing and wastewater may themselves, under certain conditions, become radiation hazards. Wastewater must be controlled to prevent further spread of contamination.

(b) Contaminated clothing and wastewater should be treated as radioactive hazards. An appropriate OEG should be set for units conducting thorough decontamination operations (i.e., consider the decontamination operation a separate mission with its own OEG).

Level of Radiological Risk

Probability / Severity	Frequent	Likely	Occasional	Seldom	Unlikely
Catastrophic	Extremely High	Extremely High	High	High	Moderate
Critical	Extremely High	High	High	Moderate	Low
Marginal	High	Moderate	Moderate	Low	Low
Negligible	Moderate	Low	Low	Low	Low

Figure D-5. Level of Radiological Risk

(4) Radiological risk management applies to patient movement missions and health care providers; however, medical treatment or lifesaving measures take precedence over decontamination efforts.

(a) Mission OEG should be established for medical missions; however, careful consideration must be given before evacuation or treatment for a contaminated individual to avoid exceeding the OEG for evacuation crews and/or health care personnel. It is highly unlikely that a contaminated patient will create a significant radiation hazard for health care providers. In most cases, removing the outer layer of clothing will eliminate most of the radioactive contamination and general medical precautions are sufficient to protect medical personnel from the radiological hazard.

(b) Treatment of radioactively contaminated casualties triaged as "immediate" should not be delayed for decontamination beyond removal of the outer layer of clothing. Decontamination can be safely delayed until immediate lifesaving actions have been accomplished and the delay/interference of decontamination will not threaten any personnel.

(5) Radiological risk management applies to all ground, air, and sea transportation missions. Risk to the transportation personnel, crew, and the mission requirements are factored into the decision process when setting the OEG. If transporting radioactive material, both the cargo and any other potential ionizing radiation exposure should be

Recommended Operational Exposure Guidance Levels

Acceptable Risk Level \ Mission Importance	Critical	Priority	Routine
Extremely High	125	75	25
High	75	25	5
Moderate	25	5	0.5
Low	5	2.5	0.5

NOTE:
The commander has the authority to select any operational exposure guidance deemed appropriate, including exceeding 125 centi-Gray, if the circumstances warrant it.

Figure D-6. Recommended Operational Exposure Guidance Levels

evaluated in the risk management process. For radioactively contaminated cargo, the decontamination requirement should be evaluated as part of the risk management process. Depending on the cargo and the mission, the OEG for the crew and transportation personnel may make decontamination unnecessary. Planning for intertheater transportation missions must consider the radiological control requirements at the destination. An intermediate intratheater stop may be required to conform to HN and international transportation requirements. Consult the memorandum from the Under Secretary of Defense, Subject: *Radiological Clearance Criteria Guidelines for Platforms and Materiel,* dated 16 December 2011, before transporting radiologically contaminated materiel out of theater.

f. Determining Decontamination Requirements

(1) Immediate or operational decontamination should be completed to reduce the possibility that residual contamination exceeds the OEG. Once the mission is completed or before beginning a new mission, thorough decontamination may be necessary to avoid additional exposure and/or exceed any newly established OEG and to keep exposure ALARA.

(2) Title 49, Code of Federal Regulations, parts 172 and 173, and Nuclear Regulatory Commission Regulatory Guide 1.86, *Termination of Operating Licenses for Nuclear Reactors,* provide guidance during peacetime environments for movement, disposal, and release of radiologically contaminated equipment and buildings for unrestricted use within the US.

(3) Under most conditions, up to 10 times background, typically averaging ~2 micro-Gray/hour, is usually considered an acceptable operating environment.

5. Additional Exposure Guidance

a. Internal uptake of radioactive material can contribute a significant dose to an individual, possibly impacting the risk management process. Internal uptake can be precluded by the use of IPE or COLPRO, but this mitigation measure is not always practical or may not be the most effective approach in reducing total risk. Internal dose assessment should be performed by a trained expert (see paragraph 6, "Service Resources"), with the following general considerations:

(1) Exposure can be assessed from nasal swabs (if done within one hour post exposure for certain radionuclides).

(2) Assessed via bioassay (blood, urine, feces, sputum) as soon as possible. Bioassay is the determination of the relative strength of a substance (as a drug) by comparing its effect on a test organism with that of a standard preparation. This normally requires special analysis by a qualified laboratory facility [see paragraph 3.b.(3), "Laboratory Grade Capabilities"].

b. Priority should be given to nuclide identification. Alpha and beta emitting radionuclides are particularly hazardous if they are internalized.

(1) Affects internal dose assessment and treatment.

(2) Determines long-term IPE (MOPP)-level guidance.

c. Protection of Civilians and Dependents.

(1) General criteria for implementing protective actions:

(a) Threshold (i.e., acute) health effects should be avoided.

(b) The risk of delayed effects should not exceed a level that is judged to be adequately protective of health in emergency situations.

(c) The risk from a protective action should not exceed the risk associated with the dose that is to be avoided.

(2) Local commanders need to coordinate with local authorities, in accordance with status-of-forces agreements and locally published guidance, to establish appropriate guidance for the protection of dependents and civilians.

(3) For additional information on intervention levels for the protection of the public during domestic and foreign situations see:

(a) The *National Response Framework* for domestic response guidance and information.

(b) NATO STANAGs, International Atomic Energy Agency safety series documents, and foreign consequence management doctrine for foreign operations.

6. Service Resources

In addition to the Service resources already identified for personnel dosimetry and radioanalytical laboratory services, each Service has uniformed and civilian radiation safety experts (health physicists) and dedicated radiation safety agencies. Service-specific identification and contact information follows:

a. US Army
Expert: Nuclear Medical Science Officer
Agency: AIPH Health Physics Program
Address: USAPHC
ATTN: MCHB-TS-OHP
5158 Blackhawk Road
Aberdeen Proving Ground, MD 21010-5403
E-mail: chppm-hpp-webrequest@amedd.army.mil
Phone: 410-436-8396
DSN: 584-8396

b. US Navy
Expert: Radiological Health Officer
Agency: Navy and Marine Corps Public Health Center
Address: 620 John Paul Jones Circle, Suite 1100
Portsmouth, VA 23708-2103
Phone: 757-953-0765 (Radiological Component Manager)
DSN: 377-0765

c. US Air Force
Expert: Bioenvironmental Engineer
Agency: US Air Force School of Aerospace Medicine
Address: 2510 5th Street, Building 840
Wright-Patterson AFB, OH 45433-7913
e-mail: usafsam.be.consultants@wpafb.af.mil
Phone: 937-938-2716
DSN: 798-2716

d. Supplemental US Air Force resource contact information:

(1) ESOH Service Center
E-mail: esoh.service.center@wpafb.af.mil
Toll Free: 1-888-232-ESOH (3764)
Phone: 937-938-3764
DSN: 798-3764
Fax: 937-656-8637

(2) Scientific and Technical Information Office
Phone: 210-536-2050
DSN: 240-2050

APPENDIX E
CONTAMINATION MITIGATION CONSIDERATIONS

1. General

The hazards associated with CBRN incidents can force US forces into protective equipment, thereby degrading their ability to perform individual and collective tasks. CCMD staffs plan, prepare for, and provide support to contamination mitigation operations and for redeployment of platforms and material to home stations once hostilities cease. Contamination mitigation includes the planning and initiation of actions that will enable the force to continue operations despite threats and hazards from CBRN material through the conduct of contamination control and medical countermeasures that allow for quick recovery.

2. Terminology

a. **Forms of Contamination (Figure E-1).** CBRN contamination is the deposition on or absorption of CBRN materials by personnel, materiel, structures, and terrain. US forces may encounter CBRN contamination through direct attack, movement through contaminated areas, the unwitting use of contaminated facilities, or the movement of vapor clouds.

b. Levels of decontamination (Figure E-2) are immediate, operational, thorough, and clearance. Immediate and operational decontamination operations are typically conducted at the tactical level in order to sustain combat operations. Thorough decontamination is normally done within the rear area. Clearance decontamination operations are normally conducted post hostilities using theater or higher-level assets in order to stabilize transition of contaminated forces for redeployment.

c. **Methods of Decontamination (Figure E-3).** Decontamination is accomplished by neutralization, physical removal, and weathering.

For further guidance, see FM 3-11.5/MCWP 3-37.3/NTTP 3-11.26/AFTTP(I) 3-2.60, Multi-Service Tactics, Techniques, and Procedures for Chemical, Biological, Radiological, and Nuclear Decontamination.

3. Considerations for Decontamination Operations

a. **Capabilities.** CCDRs and their staffs should consider their decontamination equipment capability and the detection threshold levels of their sensors during planning, as necessary. This planning requirement includes identification of in-theater capabilities to include aerial ports of debarkation (APODS) and seaports of debarkation (SPODs). FM 3-11.5/MCWP 3-37.3/NTTP 3-11.26/AFTTP(I) 3-2.60, *Multi-Service Tactics, Techniques, and Procedures for Chemical, Biological, Radiological, and Nuclear Decontamination,* and the Interagency Combating Weapons of Mass Destruction Database of Responsibilities, Authorities, and Capabilities (INDRAC) System are used to identify these capabilities.

b. **Treaties and Regulations.** GCCs should review applicable treaties, laws, regulations, and agreements pertaining to their AOR, as well as understand and consider

Forms of Chemical, Biological, Radiological, and Nuclear Contamination

Form of Contamination	Description
Vapor	Can be generated by generators or bursting munitions. Vapor in an open or outdoor area will generally disperse rapidly.
Liquid	Liquid droplets can range from thick and sticky to the consistency of water. Liquids can also be disseminated as an aerosol.
Aerosol	Is a liquid or solid composed of finely divided particles suspended in a gaseous medium. Examples of common aerosols are mist, fog, and smoke. They behave much like vapors.
Solids	Forms of contamination include radioactive particles, biological spores, and dusty agents. A dusty agent is a solid agent that can be disseminated as an aerosol.

Figure E-1. Forms of Chemical, Biological, Radiological, and Nuclear Contamination

foreign government concerns for the movement of contaminated platforms and materiel. CCDRs identify relevant governmental and nongovernmental HN, international, and US entities that may affect operational decision making in moving platforms and materiel. CCDRs use this information to develop policies, standards, plans, and concepts of operation to sustain operations and restore operational capability to platforms and materiel that have been contaminated.

c. **Personnel Decontamination.** When a CBRN incident occurs and results in casualties, a mass casualty or patient decontamination operation may be required. Not all contaminated personnel may require medical attention. Those contaminated personnel that require medical attention may fall into one of the following categories:

(1) **Casualties.** Casualties consist of injured personnel that do not necessarily need treatment or admittance to an MTF. These personnel may require self-aid or buddy aid assistance or may just need to go through the decontamination process.

(2) **Patients.** These personnel will require medical treatment, life- or limb-saving care, or evacuation to the next role of care. It is important that these patients go through patient decontamination before they are admitted to the MTF. However, in some CBRN scenarios, little or no decontamination may be necessary to process a patient, especially if lifesaving measures are time critical. If transport is deemed essential, all efforts must be made to prevent the spread of contamination. In these cases, prior approval must be given by the Commander, United States Transportation Command (CDRUSTRANSCOM) and SecDef in consultation with DOD medical authorities.

Levels of Chemical, Biological, Radiological, and Nuclear Decontamination

Level of Decontamination	Description
Immediate Decontamination	Immediate decontamination carried out by individuals immediately upon becoming contaminated to save lives, minimize casualties, and limit the spread or transfer of contamination.
Operational Decontamination	Decontamination carried out by an individual and/or a unit, restricted to specific parts of operationally essential equipment, materiel, and/or working areas, in order to minimize contact and transfer hazards and to sustain operations.
Thorough Decontamination	This is accomplished by units (with or without external support) to reduce contamination on personnel, equipment, materiel, and/or working areas equal to natural background or to the lowest possible levels, to permit the partial or total removal of individual protective equipment and to maintain operations with minimum degradation.
Clearance Decontamination	The final level of decontamination that provides the decontamination of equipment and personnel to a level that allows unrestricted transportation, maintenance, employment, and disposal.

Figure E-2. Levels of Chemical, Biological, Radiological, and Nuclear Decontamination

For further guidance on casualty and patient decontamination, see FM 4-02.7/MCRP 4-11.1F/NTTP 4-02.7/AFTTP 3-42.3, Multi-Service Tactics, Techniques, and Procedures for Health Service Support in a Chemical, Biological, Radiological, and Nuclear Environment, *current USTRANSCOM policies, and JP 4-02,* Health Services.

d. **Logistics.** Planning considerations are Service dependent; however, where possible theater bulk reserves/stocks should be planned in order to facilitate resupply.

For more information on logistics, see JP 4-0, Joint Logistics. *For more information on decontamination operations, see FM 3-11.5/MCWP 3-37.3/NTTP 3-11.26/AFTTP(I) 3-2.60,* Multi-Service Tactics, Techniques, and Procedures for Chemical, Biological, Radiological, and Nuclear Decontamination.

e. **Guidelines for Formerly Contaminated Platforms and Materiel**

(1) Formerly contaminated platforms and materiel that undergo thorough decontamination may be used to meet mission requirements, but under restricted use. They remain under USG control and are restricted to DOD-controlled facilities, unless cleared by partner nations (for locations outside the US).

(2) When mission requirements allow, formerly contaminated platforms and materiel are decontaminated to clearance criteria (unrestricted operations). These measures ensure formerly contaminated platforms and materiel do not present a health risk. Platforms

Methods of Chemical, Biological, Radiological, and Nuclear Decontamination	
Methods of Decontamination	**Description**
Neutralization	Is the most widely used method of decontamination, particularly for chemical warfare agents. Neutralization is the reaction of the contaminating agent with other chemicals to render the agent less toxic or nontoxic.
Physical Removal	Is the relocation of the contamination from one mission-critical surface to another less important location. Physical removal generally leaves the contamination in toxic form. It often involves the subsequent neutralization of the contamination.
Weathering	Involves such processes as evaporation and irradiation to remove or destroy the contaminant. The contaminated item is exposed to natural elements (e.g., sun, wind, heat, precipitation) to dilute or destroy the contaminant to the point of reduced or negligible hazard.

Figure E-3. Methods of Chemical, Biological, Radiological, and Nuclear Decontamination

and materiel that are not decontaminated to clearance criteria and approved for transit should not depart the theater of operations without authorization from USTRANSCOM and in coordination with the affected CCDR and SecDef. DOS is the approval authority for platforms porting in areas outside the US in coordination with those countries at which the platforms are porting. The approval authority for porting locations within the US is SecDef after obtaining the President's approval, in consultation with appropriate federal and state agencies. Clearance standards for DOD, national, and international agencies may vary. Consult appropriate authority.

(3) CCDRs use clearance criteria guidelines established by the Office of the Under Secretary of Defense and current national/international guidelines. When more than one standard is presented, the more conservative approach should be taken. Complete elimination of CBRN contaminants from platforms and materiel may not be possible due to limitations in currently fielded technologies and procedures. Furthermore, chemical agents absorb into porous materials such as rubber, plastic, and cloth and may become an "off-gasing" or contact hazard even after decontamination operations are complete.

(4) Documentation of the certified clearance level decontamination should be maintained and tracked in the appropriate maintenance records physically maintained for the platforms and/or materiel.

See FM 3-11.34/MCWP 3-37.5/NTTP 3-11.23/AFTTP(I) 3-2.33, Multi-Service Tactics, Techniques, and Procedures for Installation CBRN Defense, *for additional information for the retrograde movement of decontaminated equipment.*

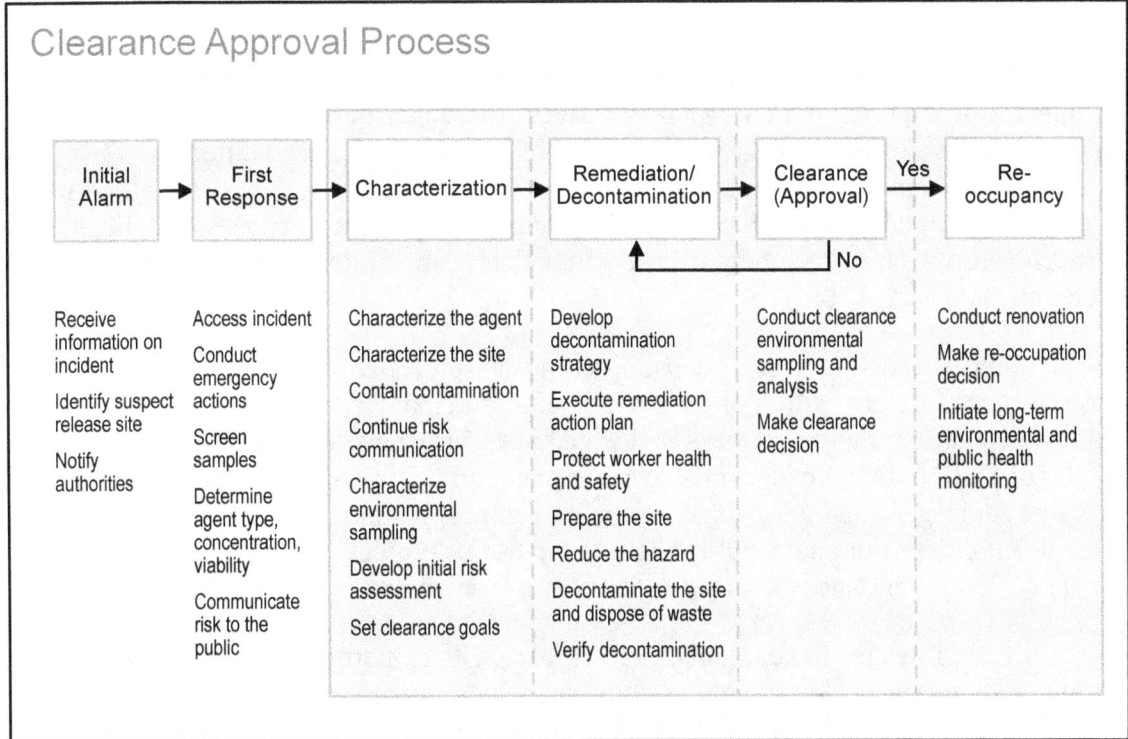

Figure E-4. Clearance Approval Process

f. **Clearance Approval Process.** Figure E-4 illustrates the step-by-step process leading to approval to reoccupy the platform or use/transport materiel. Clearance criteria are the processes and measured levels by which decontamination efforts are considered acceptable for the restoration to routine use of a platform and materiel by unprotected personnel. By achieving clearance decontamination, unprotected civilians may conduct routine maintenance, fueling, inspections, loading/unloading, or similar activities. Passengers may include members of the non-DOD general population following clearance decontamination. The assumptions are as follows:

(1) The JFC or GCC has the capabilities required to identify the presence of a CBRN contamination hazard and to determine whether the hazard has been effectively mitigated;

(2) DOD will have the policy, standards, and protocols required to assess and characterize contamination;

(3) The source, type, and amount of contamination have been characterized;

(4) The hazard has been reduced to an acceptable exposure level; and

(5) The asset will be used by unprotected persons, except for depot-level maintenance activities.

4. Additional Sustainment Considerations

a. Operations will slow as tasks are performed by personnel encumbered by protective equipment or exposed to CBRN hazard effects. Hazards may require abandonment or limited use of contaminated areas, transfer of missions to uncontaminated forces, or avoidance of planned terrain and routes. Additionally, CBRN use or contamination resulting in a major disruption of normal personnel and materiel replacement processes in the theater could severely hamper the component commanders' capabilities for force generation and sustainment.

(1) Theater sustainment capabilities must be protected. CBRN contamination at an essential port of embarkation or port of debarkation or other critical logistic facility can significantly affect campaign plans and execution. Measures to prevent and mitigate the effects of CBRN contamination must focus on maintaining support to combat operations and rapidly restoring the degraded capabilities. Preventing and mitigating the effects of CBRN hazards on equipment and supplies include the use of protective coatings and coverings. Under some circumstances it may be necessary to use alternative facilities.

(2) Protecting forces from the effects of a CBRN environment is logistically taxing. Resupply requirements for protective clothing, medical supplies (antidotes, antibiotics, and antivirals), and sustainment supplies for quarantine/isolation facilities will be time-sensitive. Low-density CBRN protective equipment may require movement within the theater. Personnel and equipment decontamination requires a great amount of water, which becomes contaminated in the process. These and other resources needed for recovery from CBRN incidents can severely strain the theater logistic system and have unanticipated effects on combat operations.

(3) Logistic Planning Considerations for Fixed Sites. Ports, airfields, and related fixed sites are choke points vulnerable to CBRN incidents and potentially high-value targets. Combat forces are vulnerable to CBRN incidents during entry operations and during movement to areas of military operations. Common fixed site defense measures can reduce their vulnerability.

(a) Considerations for APODs. While each APOD is unique, a few general considerations are important. When considering CBRN threats, the installation's overall size with respect to the mission and its operational capacity and flexibility will affect the commander's options for decontamination and avoidance. However, conducting successful attacks against APODs presents significant challenges to the adversary. If installation leadership and personnel are properly prepared to survive the attack and sustain operations, CBRN attacks may not cause significant long-term degradation of throughput capacity, unless the attack is nuclear or involves a biological agent that remains undetected until it has spread through a significant portion of critical personnel and/or equipment. This is especially true at large APODs where critical assets and much of the storage areas and MHE could easily escape contamination. Operations in these cases may be limited more by the effects of the attacks on the local work force and nearby civilian population. In most cases, it will be possible to continue operations at a contaminated APOD. While CBRN incidents may result in contamination of some operating surfaces, the size of the hazard area may be small compared to the size of the installation. The capability to quickly shift operations to those areas and facilities on the installation that were not contaminated is key to sustaining throughput operations.

1. If necessary, contaminated aircraft must be decontaminated to the level required by DOD and the HN, and acceptable to the International Civil Aviation Organization, before returning to the air mobility flow. The GCC is responsible for establishing control of contaminated aircraft in the AOR and at designated decontamination sites, and for procedures to address overflight requirements and destination base/country landing rights for previously contaminated aircraft.

2. In CBRN environments, there are limitations on the employment of aircraft. Some aircraft will not be able to land at or depart from contaminated areas regardless of an aerial port's CBRN preparedness. Of particular importance are the Civil Reserve Air Fleet, civilian, and other aircraft under contract to support military operations. CCMD plans must provide for replacing these aircraft with other airlift assets or conducting transload operations from bases outside the immediate threat area. These replacement aircraft would have to operate from transload airbases to shuttle the affected cargo and passengers to the theater. If that is not feasible, alternative means (e.g., sea, rail, or wheeled transport) must be made available.

3. The availability of alternative aerial ports to accomplish the transload of personnel and materiel from intertheater to intratheater airlift can minimize potential deployment interruptions by adversary CBRN use. The supported CCDR, in coordination with the CDRUSTRANSCOM, is responsible for designating transload aerial ports. All means of active and passive contamination avoidance measures will minimize the level of contamination and will prevent further cross-contamination during operations.

(b) Considerations for Seaports of Embarkation. JFC plans must take into account MSC ships exposed to contamination. Contaminated ships will require decontamination support and certification acceptable to civil authorities in order to load additional cargo at uncontaminated US or foreign commercial port facilities.

(c) Considerations for SPODs. In large-scale operations, US equipment and material normally enter the theater on strategic sealift ships and offload at SPODs. The vital importance of these seaports to US power projection makes them an attractive target for CBRN incidents. However, conducting successful attacks against SPODs presents significant challenges to the adversary. If port managers and operators are properly prepared to survive the attack and sustain operations, CBRN attacks may not cause significant long-term degradation of military logistic capacity. This is especially true at large ports where many piers, storage areas, and much of the MHE may escape contamination. Operations in these cases may be limited more by the effects of the attacks on the local work force and nearby civilian populations.

1. Though similarities concerning the impact of CBRN attack on SPOD and APOD operations exist, there are differences. For example, assignment of overall responsibility for decontamination efforts is more complex.

2. Each port provides unique capabilities and has different vulnerabilities in CBRN environments, but contamination avoidance is an essential element of sustaining operations. In normal circumstances, a port is but one node of a complex, theater-wide logistic network. Plans should include options for redirecting incoming ships when possible from contaminated ports to those that are uncontaminated. However, when alternative ports with adequate capacity and berths to handle large cargo ships are not available, it may be necessary to continue operations at contaminated ports. In considering alternative ports, planners must take into account the requirements for unit equipment to arrive in proximity to the marshalling areas for unit personnel, ammunition, and sustainment supplies in order to ensure coherent RSOI for affected units.

3. In some cases, it will be possible to continue operations at a contaminated port. While CBRN incidents may result in contamination of some operating surfaces, the size of the contaminated area may be small compared to the size of the port. The capability to shift operations to those areas and facilities within the port that escaped contamination is key to sustaining throughput operations. Proper preparation can significantly reduce the impact of CBRN incidents on a SPOD.

b. Specific sustaining considerations include:

(1) Decontaminating critical areas or facilities.

(2) Determining the disposition of contaminated equipment, facilities, and human remains.

(3) Coordinating salvage and decontamination of materials.

(4) Providing C2 of restoration operations.

(5) Integrating CBRN incident restoration operations.

(6) Providing restoration country assistance teams.

(7) Establishing reporting procedures for restoration requirements.

(8) Providing operational guidance to contaminated forces.

(9) Assessing the operational impact of restoration activities, to include assessing the linkage of restoration and the operational risk assessment.

(10) Supporting restoration of SOF operations.

(11) Establishing contamination control.

(12) Working with HN.

(a) Supplying or pre-positioning protective consumable, expendable, and replacement CBRN equipment.

(b) Employing protective measures to minimize the effects of CBRN incidents.

(c) Integrating multinational and US protective measures and assets.

(d) Establishing appropriate CBRN medical protection measures.

(e) Providing COLPRO for C2, medical operations, and work force rest and relief.

(f) Implementing effective ROM, to include social distancing, isolation, and quarantine as appropriate, to limit exposure following a CBRN incident.

Intentionally Blank

APPENDIX F
TECHNICAL CHEMICAL, BIOLOGICAL, RADIOLOGICAL, AND NUCLEAR FORCES

1. This appendix introduces technical CBRN force capabilities and some planning considerations for their use during operations in support of operational and strategic-level objectives where CBRN hazards exist.

2. It is imperative that the JFC and those responsible for apportioning forces and developing support plans not only understand the unique capabilities but also the limitations of technical CBRN forces within their operational areas prior to a CBRN or CWMD incident or mission.

3. Technical CBRN forces include specialized capabilities that are organized, equipped, and trained to conduct CBRN operations beyond the tactical level and in support of operational and strategic objectives to counter WMD. Technical CBRN forces are generally low density and high demand, and require significant mission prioritization in order to meet the requirements of a joint campaign. They possess advanced capabilities to identify CBRN threats and hazards with a high degree of confidence necessary to drive command decisions above the tactical level, to include providing evidence collection for attribution and the employment of medical countermeasures. Technical CBRN forces operate across the range of military operations and are able to integrate with joint, interagency, and multinational partners as part of a much larger effort. Below is a list of the DOD's technical CBRN forces and the references for additional information on them:

   a. Chemical reconnaissance detachment (CRD) (for more information on CRDs, see Appendix A of ATP 3-11.24, *Technical CBRNE Operations*).

   b. Chemical decontamination detachment (CDD) (for more information on CDDs, see Appendix B of ATP 3-11.24, *Technical CBRNE Operations*).

   c. Decontamination and reconnaissance teams (DRTs) (for more information on DRTs, see Appendix C of ATP 3-11.24, *Technical CBRNE Operations*).

   d. Weapons of mass destruction coordination element (WCE) (for more information on WCE, see Appendix D of ATP 3-11.24, *Technical CBRNE Operations*).

   e. Nuclear disablement teams (NDTs) (for more information on NDTs, see Appendix E of ATP 3-11.24, *Technical CBRNE Operations*).

   f. Weapons of mass destruction-civil support teams (WMD-CSTs) (for more information on WMD-CSTs, see Appendix F of ATP 3-11.24, *Technical CBRNE Operations*).

   g. CBRNE response teams (CRTs) (for more information on CRTs, see Appendix G of ATP 3-11.24, *Technical CBRNE Operations*).

   h. CBRNE analytical and remediation activity (CARA) (for more information on CARA, see Appendix H of ATP 3-11.24, *Technical CBRNE Operations*).

i. Laboratory support (for more information on supporting laboratories, see Appendix I of ATP 3-11.24, *Technical CBRNE Operations*, as well as Chapter 6 and Appendix H of ATP 3-11.37/MCWP 3-37.4/NTTP 3-11.29/AFTTP 3-2.44, *Multi-Service Tactics, Techniques, and Procedures for Chemical, Biological, Radiological, and Nuclear Reconnaissance and Surveillance*).

j. Marine air-ground task force (MAGTF) CBRN assessment and consequence management teams (for more information on MAGTF CBRN assessment and consequence management teams, see Chapter 5 of MCWP 3-37, *Marine Air-Ground Task Force Chemical, Biological, Radiological, and Nuclear Support to Combat Weapons of Mass Destruction*, and Appendix K of ATTP 3-11.36/MCRP 3-37B/NTTP 3-11.34/AFTTP 3-2.70, *Multi-Service Tactics, Techniques, and Procedures for Chemical, Biological, Radiological, and Nuclear Aspects of Command and Control*).

k. Chemical Biological Incident Response Force (CBIRF) (for more information on CBIRF, see Chapter 8 of MCWP 3-37, *Marine Air-Ground Task Force Chemical, Biological, Radiological, and Nuclear Support to Combating Weapons of Mass Destruction*, and Appendix K of ATTP 3-11.36/MCRP 3-37B/NTTP 3-11.34/AFTTP 3-2.70, *Multi-Service Tactics, Techniques, and Procedures for Chemical, Biological, Radiological, and Nuclear Aspects of Command and Control*).

l. US Air Force CBRN/emergency management hazard assessment team and installation management team for military operations in a CBRN, major accident response, or natural disaster environment. (For more information, see AFMAN 10-2503, *Operations in a Chemical, Biological, Radiological, Nuclear, and High-Yield Explosive [CBRNE]) Environment*, and ATTP 3-11.36/MCRP 3-37B/NTTP 3-11.34/AFTTP 3-2.70, *Multi-Service Tactics, Techniques, and Procedures for Chemical, Biological, Radiological, and Nuclear Aspects of Command and Control*).

m. US Air Force CBRN/emergency management superintendent and air operations center manager for operations at the installation, warfighting headquarters, combined/joint task force or major command level (for more information, see AFMAN 10-2503, *Operations in a Chemical, Biological, Radiological, Nuclear, and High-Yield Explosive [CBRNE] Environment*, and ATTP 3-11.36/MCRP 3-37B/NTTP 3-11.34/AFTTP 3-2.70, *Multi-Service Tactics, Techniques, and Procedures for Chemical, Biological, Radiological, and Nuclear Aspects of Command and Control*).

n. US Army Nuclear and Combating Weapons of Mass Destruction Agency nuclear employment augmentation teams and CWMD planning assistance teams (for more information, see Army Regulation 10-16, *US Army Nuclear and Combating Weapons of Mass Destruction Agency*).

4. The Marine Corps provides forces in support of joint CWMD operations with a variety of capabilities. Some of these Marine Corps CWMD capabilities require specialized manning, training, and equipping peculiar to the CWMD operation. Many other Marine Corps CWMD contributions are core MAGTF capabilities that can be utilized with adaptations to support joint force CWMD requirements.

a. The Marine Corps provides forces to support CWMD operations with a variety of capabilities. However, not all of the CWMD military mission areas are the focus or priority for Marine Corps forces. Through all military mission areas, Marine Corps forces are prepared to support the C2 requirements for joint forces conducting CWMD operations. MCWP 3-37, *Marine Air-Ground Task Force Chemical, Biological, Radiological, and Nuclear Support to Combating Weapons of Mass Destruction*, provides a basic outline of the types of support that Marine Corps forces can provide in each mission area, the nature of likely command relationships of Marine Corps forces to joint forces, and the initial assessed level of focus for the Marine Corps to support each CWMD mission area, recognizing other forces and agencies have primary responsibility in certain mission areas.

b. MAGTF operations include the employment of tactical capabilities that counter the entire range of CBRN threats and hazards through the capabilities of WMD proliferation prevention, WMD counterforce, CBRN defense, and CBRN CM when applied in support of operational and strategic objectives to combat WMD and operate safely in CBRN environments.

5. SOF have a role primarily in nonproliferation and counterproliferation by providing expertise, materiel, and teams to support CCMDs to locate, tag, and track WMD; conduct interdiction and other offensive operations in limited areas as required; build partnership capacity for conducting counterproliferation activities; conduct military information support operations to dissuade adversary reliance on WMD; and other specialized technical capabilities, including technical reachback capabilities. Although SOF also have a unique role in CWMD and operating in a CBRN environment, they cannot fully operate under CBRN threat conditions or conduct SOF-specific CWMD missions without the assistance of conventional forces. For example, while SOF also have limited organic CBRN decontamination, reconnaissance, and sensitive site exploitation capability, they lack the capacity to conduct long-term sustainment and reconstitution operations without large-scale logistical resupply.

For more detailed information on SOF capabilities and limitations, see United States Special Operations Command (USSOCOM) Publication 3-11, Multi-Service Tactics, Techniques, and Procedures for Special Operations Forces in Nuclear, Biological, and Chemical Environments, *and USSOCOM Publication 1,* Doctrine for Special Operations.

6. The US Strategic Command (USSTRATCOM) has overall responsibility for synchronization of CWMD planning, supported by USSOCOM as the lead CCMD for operations against terrorist use of WMD. The USSTRATCOM Center for Combating WMD, in conjunction with DTRA, maintains the INDRAC System as a Web-based strategic-level reference resource listing the CWMD roles, authorities, and capabilities of DOD and other USG departments and agencies. INDRAC is validated by the referenced USG departments and agencies, contains technical CBRN force capabilities information and is accessible to USG authorized users on both the Nonsecure Internet Protocol Router Network (NIPRNET) (http://indrac.dtra.mil) and the SECRET Internet Protocol Router Network (SIPRNET) (https://indrac.dtra.smil.mil). Additionally, DTRA is the single source point of contact for technical reachback requests for information at:

DTRA Operations Center, 24/7 Contact
Phone: 1-877-240-1187 or 703-767-2000 or 703-767-2003
DSN: 427-2000 or 427-2003
Unclassified fax: 703-767-2094
Classified fax: 703-767-2085
E-mail: opscntr1@dtra.mil
Web site; http://www.dtra.mil/Missions/Reachback/OPSCenter.aspx

7. United States Coast Guard (USCG) forces conduct operations under USCG authorities or when assigned to DOD commanders. The USCG deploys expeditionary forces to support overseas GCCs. Select USCG deployable specialized forces have advanced CBRN technical capabilities. These include the USCG Maritime Security Response Team (MSRT) and the USCG National Strike Force (NSF). The MSRT may operate in an opposed environment while NSF forces operate in a permissive environment. NSF forces may serve as, or support, the designated federal on-scene coordinator for a hazardous material incident.

APPENDIX G
REFERENCES

The development of JP 3-11 is based upon the following primary references:

1. Strategic Guidance and Policy

a. Homeland Security Presidential Directive (HSPD)-5, *Management of Domestic Incidents.*

b. HSPD-18, *Medical Countermeasures Against Weapons of Mass Destruction.*

c. Memorandum from the Under Secretary of Defense, Subject: *Radiological Clearance Criteria Guidelines for Platforms and Materiel,* 16 December 2011.

d. National Security Presidential Directive (NSPD)-17/HSPD-4, *National Strategy to Combat Weapons of Mass Destruction.*

e. NSPD-33/HSPD-10, *Biodefense for the 21st Century.*

f. NSPD-46/HSPD-15, *US Policy and Strategy in the War on Terror[ism].*

g. *National Defense Strategy of the United States of America.*

h. *National Military Strategy.*

i. *National Military Strategy to Combat Weapons of Mass Destruction.*

j. *National Response Framework.*

k. *National Security Strategy.*

l. *The National Strategy for Biological Surveillance.*

m. *National Strategy for Homeland Security.*

n. Presidential Decision Directive/National Security Council 60, *Nuclear Weapons Employment Policy Guidance.*

o. Presidential Policy Directive 8, *National Preparedness.*

p. *Strategy for Homeland Defense and Civil Support.*

2. Department of Defense Publications

a. Department of Defense Directive (DODD) 3025.18, *Defense Support of Civil Authorities (DSCA).*

b. DODD 3150.08, *DOD Response to Nuclear and Radiological Incidents.*

c. DODD 5100.46, *Foreign Disaster Relief (FDR)*.

d. DODI 2000.12, *DOD Antiterrorism (AT) Program*.

e. DODI 2000.21, *Foreign Consequence Management (FCM)*.

f. DODI 3020.52, *DOD Installation Chemical, Biological, Radiological, Nuclear, and High-Yield Explosive (CBRNE) Preparedness Standards*.

g. DODI 6055.08, *Occupational Ionizing Radiation Protection Program*.

h. DODI 6055.1, *DOD Safety and Occupational Health (SOH) Program*.

i. DODI 6055.17, *DOD Installation Emergency Management (IEM) Program*.

j. DODI 6200.03, *Public Health Emergency Management Within the Department of Defense*.

k. DODI 6490.03, *Deployment Health*.

l. *Department of Defense Foreign Clearance Manual* (https://www.fcg.pentagon.mil).

m. Armed Forces Radiobiology Research Institute, *Medical Management of Radiological Casualties*, 3rd edition.

3. Chairman of the Joint Chiefs of Staff Publications

a. CJCS Concept Plan 0500, *Military Assistance to Domestic Consequence Management Operations in Response to a Chemical, Biological, Radiological, Nuclear, or High-Yield Explosives Situation*.

b. Chairman of the Joint Chiefs of Staff Instruction (CJCSI) 2030.01C, *Chemical Weapons Convention Compliance Policy Guidance*.

c. CJCSI 2700.01E, *International Military Agreements for Rationalization, Standardization, and Interoperability (RSI) Between the United States, Its Allies, and Other Friendly Nations*.

d. CJCSI 3125.01C, *Defense Response to Chemical, Biological, Radiological, and Nuclear (CBRN) Incidents in the Homeland*.

e. CJCSI 3214.01D, *Defense Support for Chemical, Biological, Radiological, and Nuclear Incidents on Foreign Territory*.

f. CJCSI 3431.01C, *Joint Nuclear Accident and Incident Response Team*.

g. Chairman of the Joint Chiefs of Staff Manual (CJCSM) 3122.01A, *Joint Operation Planning and Execution System (JOPES) Volume I, Planning Policies and Procedures*.

h. CJCSM 3130.03, *Adaptive Planning and Execution (APEX) Planning Formats and Guidance.*

4. **Joint Publications**

a. JP 1, *Doctrine for the Armed Forces of the United States.*

b. JP 1-0, *Joint Personnel Support.*

c. JP 1-02, *Department of Defense Dictionary of Military and Associated Terms.*

d. JP 1-05, *Religious Affairs in Joint Operations.*

e. JP 2-0, *Joint Intelligence.*

f. JP 2-01.3, *Joint Intelligence Preparation of the Operational Environment.*

g. JP 3-0, *Joint Operations.*

h. JP 3-08, *Interorganizational Coordination During Joint Operations.*

i. JP 3-10, *Joint Security Operations in Theater.*

j. JP 3-13, *Information Operations.*

k. JP 3-27, *Homeland Defense.*

l. JP 3-28, *Defense Support of Civil Authorities.*

m. JP 3-29, *Foreign Humanitarian Assistance.*

n. JP 3-33, *Joint Task Force Headquarters.*

o. JP 3-35, *Deployment and Redeployment Operations.*

p. JP 3-40, *Countering Weapons of Mass Destruction.*

q. JP 3-41, *Chemical, Biological, Radiological, and Nuclear Consequence Management.*

r. JP 3-61, *Public Affairs.*

s. JP 4-0, *Joint Logistics.*

t. JP 4-02, *Health Services..*

u. JP 4-06, *Mortuary Affairs.*

v. JP 5-0, *Joint Operation Planning.*

w. JP 6-0, *Joint Communications System.*

5. Multi-Service Publications

a. ATP 3-11.37/MCWP 3-37.4/NTTP 3-11.29/AFTTP 3-2.44, *Multi-Service Tactics, Techniques, and Procedures for Chemical, Biological, Radiological, and Nuclear Reconnaissance and Surveillance.*

b. ATP 4-02.84/MCRP 4-11.1C/NTRP 4-02.23/AFMAN 44-156 IP, *Multi-Service Tactics, Techniques, and Procedures for the Treatment of Biological Warfare Agents Casualties.*

c. ATTP 3-11.36/MCRP 3-37B/NTTP 3-11.34/AFTTP 3-2.70, *Multi-Service Tactics, Techniques, and Procedures for Chemical, Biological, Radiological, and Nuclear Aspects of Command and Control.*

d. FM 3-11/MCWP 3-37.1/NWP 3-11/AFTTP 3-2.42, *Multi-Service Doctrine for Chemical, Biological, Radiological, and Nuclear Operations.*

e. FM 3-11.3/MCRP 3-37.2A/NTTP 3-11.25/AFTTP(I) 3-2.56, *Multi-Service Tactics, Techniques, and Procedures for Chemical, Biological, Radiological, and Nuclear Contamination Avoidance.*

f. FM 3-11.4/MCWP 3-37.2/NTTP 3-11.27/AFTTP(I) 3-2.46, *Multi-Service Tactics, Techniques, and Procedures for Nuclear, Biological, and Chemical (NBC) Protection.*

g. FM 3-11.5/MCWP 3-37.3/NTTP 3-11.26/AFTTP(I) 3-2.60, *Multi-Service Tactics, Techniques, and Procedures for Chemical, Biological, Radiological, and Nuclear Decontamination.*

h. FM 3-11.34/MCWP 3-37.5/NTTP 3-11.23/AFTTP(I) 3-2.33, *Multi-Service Tactics, Techniques, and Procedures for Installation CBRN Defense.*

i. FM 4-02.283/MCRP 4-11.1B/NTRP 4-02.21, *Treatment of Nuclear and Radiological Casualties.*

j. FM 4-02.7/MCRP 4-11.1F/NTTP 4-02.7/AFTTP 3-42.3, *Multi-Service Tactics, Techniques, and Procedures for Health Service Support in a Chemical, Biological, Radiological, and Nuclear Environment.*

k. NTTP/Coast Guard TTP 3-20.31, *Surface Ship Survivability.*

l. *Naval Ships Technical Manual/USCG Naval Engineering Manual Shipboard Chemical Warfare/Biological Warfare (CW/BW) Defense and Countermeasures.*

6. United States Air Force Publications

a. Air Force Policy Directive (AFPD) 10-25, *Emergency Management.*

b. AFPD 10-26, *Counter-Chemical, Biological, Radiological, and Nuclear Operations*.

c. Air Force Doctrine Document 3-40, *Counter-CBRN Operations*.

d. Air Force Instruction (AFI) 10-2501, *Air Force Emergency Management Program Planning and Operations*.

e. AFI 10-2603, *Emergency Health Powers on Air Force Installations*.

f. AFI 10-2604, *Disease Containment Planning Guidance*.

g. AFI 10-2607, *Air Force Chemical, Biological, Radiological, and Nuclear (CBRN) Survivability*.

h. AFI 34-242, *Mortuary Affairs Program*.

i. AFI 48-148, *Ionizing Radiation Protection*.

j. AFMAN 10-2503, *Operations in a Chemical, Biological, Radiological, Nuclear, and High-Yield Explosive (CBRNE) Environment*.

k. AFMAN 10-2605, *Education, Training and Exercise Competencies for Counter-CBRN Operations*.

7. Multinational Documents and Publications

a. Department of Transportation *Emergency Response Guidebook 2012*.

b. NATO Allied Medical Publication (AMedP)-6(C) Volume 1, *NATO Handbook on the Medical Aspects of NBC Defensive Operations (Nuclear)*.

c. NATO AMedP-6(C) Volume 2, *NATO Handbook on the Medical Aspects of NBC Defensive Operations (Biological)*.

d. NATO AMedP-6(C) Volume 3, *NATO Handbook on the Medical Aspects of NBC Defensive Operations (Chemical)*.

e. Allied Engineering Publication-7, *Chemical, Biological, Radiological, and Nuclear (CBRN) Defense Factors in the Design, Testing, and Acceptance of Military Equipment* (Edition 5).

f. NATO STANAG 2471 Edition 4, *Chemical, Biological, Radiological, and Nuclear (CBRN) Hazard Management for Airlift Operations*.

g. NATO STANAG 2473, *Commander's Guide to Radiation Exposures in Non-Article 5 Crisis Response Operations*.

8. United States Coast Guard Publications

    a. Commandant, United States Coast Guard, Instruction 3400.4, *Chemical, Biological, Radiological, and Nuclear (CBRN) Policy for Coast Guard Expeditionary Forces.*

    b. Coast Guard Publication 3-1, *Deployable Specialized Forces.*

APPENDIX H
ADMINISTRATIVE INSTRUCTIONS

1. User Comments

Users in the field are highly encouraged to submit comments on this publication to: Joint Staff J-7, Deputy Director, Joint Education and Doctrine, ATTN: Joint Doctrine Analysis Division, 116 Lake View Parkway, Suffolk, VA 23435-2697. These comments should address content (accuracy, usefulness, consistency, and organization), writing, and appearance.

2 Authorship

The lead agent for this publication is the US Army. The Joint Staff doctrine sponsor for this publication is the Director, Joint Requirements Office for Chemical, Biological, Radiological, and Nuclear Defense for Strategic Plans and Policy (J-8).

3. Supersession

This publication supersedes JP 3-11, 26 August 2008, *Joint Doctrine for Operations in Nuclear, Biological, and Chemical (NBC) Environments.*

4. Change Recommendations

a. Recommendations for urgent changes to this publication should be submitted:

TO: JOINT STAFF WASHINGTON DC//J7-JE&D//

b. Routine changes should be submitted electronically to the Deputy Director, Joint Education and Doctrine, ATTN: Joint Doctrine Analysis Division, 116 Lake View Parkway, Suffolk, VA 23435-2697, and info the lead agent and the Director for Joint Force Development, J-7/JE&D.

c. When a Joint Staff directorate submits a proposal to the CJCS that would change source document information reflected in this publication, that directorate will include a proposed change to this publication as an enclosure to its proposal. The Services and other organizations are requested to notify the Joint Staff J-7 when changes to source documents reflected in this publication are initiated.

5. Distribution of Publications

Local reproduction is authorized and access to unclassified publications is unrestricted. However, access to and reproduction authorization for classified JPs must be IAW DOD Manual 5200.01, Volume 1, *DOD Information Security Program: Overview, Classification, and Declassification,* and DOD Manual 5200.01, Volume 3, *DOD Information Security Program: Protection of Classified Information.*

6. Distribution of Electronic Publications

a. Joint Staff J-7 will not print copies of JPs for distribution. Electronic versions are available on JDEIS at https://jdeis.js.mil (NIPRNET) and http://jdeis.js.smil.mil (SIPRNET), and on the JEL at http://www.dtic.mil/doctrine (NIPRNET).

b. Only approved JPs are releasable outside the CCMDs, Services, and Joint Staff. Release of any classified JP to foreign governments or foreign nationals must be requested through the local embassy (Defense Attaché Office) to DIA, Defense Foreign Liaison/IE-3, 200 MacDill Blvd., Joint Base Anacostia-Bolling, Washington, DC 20340-5100.

c. JEL CD-ROM. Upon request of a joint doctrine development community member, the Joint Staff J-7 will produce and deliver one CD-ROM with current JPs. This JEL CD-ROM will be updated not less than semi-annually and when received can be locally reproduced for use within the CCMDs, Services, and combat support agencies.

GLOSSARY
PART I—ABBREVIATIONS AND ACRONYMS

AFI	Air Force instruction
AFMAN	Air Force manual
AFPD	Air Force policy directive
AFTTP	Air Force tactics, techniques, and procedures
AFTTP(I)	Air Force tactics, techniques, and procedures (instruction)
ALARA	as low as reasonably achievable
AMedP	allied medical publication
amu	atomic mass unit
AOI	area of interest
AOR	area of responsibility
APOD	aerial port of debarkation
ATP	Army tactical publication
ATTP	Army tactics, techniques, and procedures
BW	biological warfare
C2	command and control
CARA	chemical, biological, radiological, nuclear, and high-yield explosives analytical and remediation activity
CBIRF	Chemical-Biological Incident Response Force
CBRN	chemical, biological, radiological, and nuclear
CBRN CM	chemical, biological, radiological, and nuclear consequence management
CBRNE	chemical, biological, radiological, nuclear, and high-yield explosives
CCDR	combatant commander
CCMD	combatant command
CDD	chemical decontamination detachment
CDRUSTRANSCOM	Commander, United States Transportation Command
CJCS	Chairman of the Joint Chiefs of Staff
CJCSI	Chairman of the Joint Chiefs of Staff instruction
CJCSM	Chairman of the Joint Chiefs of Staff manual
COA	course of action
COLPRO	collective protection
CRD	chemical reconnaissance detachment
CRT	chemical, biological, radiological, nuclear, and high-yield explosives response team
CT	computed tomography
CWA	chemical warfare agent
CWC	Chemical Weapons Convention
CWMD	countering weapons of mass destruction

DOD	Department of Defense
DODD	Department of Defense directive
DODI	Department of Defense instruction
DOS	Department of State
DRT	decontamination and reconnaissance team
DTRA	Defense Threat Reduction Agency
DU	depleted uranium
EMP	electromagnetic pulse
EP	emergency preparedness
ERG	Emergency Response Guidebook
ESOH	environmental, safety, and occupational health
FM	field manual (Army)
FP	force protection
GCC	geographic combatant commander
HEMP	high-altitude electromagnetic pulse
HN	host nation
HSPD	homeland security Presidential directive
IAA	incident area assessment
IED	improvised explosive device
IGO	intergovernmental organization
IND	improvised nuclear device
INDRAC	Interagency Combating Weapons of Mass Destruction Database of Responsibilities, Authorities, and Capabilities
IPE	individual protective equipment
IRC	information-related capability
ISR	intelligence, surveillance, and reconnaissance
JFC	joint force commander
JGWE	joint global warning enterprise
JIPOE	joint intelligence preparation of the operational environment
JMAO	joint mortuary affairs office
JOPP	joint operation planning process
JP	joint publication
kph	kilometers per hour
kt	kiloton(s)
LEMP	low-altitude electromagnetic pulse
MACRMS	mortuary affairs contaminated remains mitigation site

MAGTF	Marine air-ground task force
MCRP	Marine Corps reference publication
MCWP	Marine Corps warfighting publication
MHE	materials handling equipment
MOE	measure of effectiveness
MOP	measure of performance
MOPP	mission-oriented protective posture
MSC	Military Sealift Command
MSRT	Maritime Security Response Team (USCG)
MTF	medical treatment facility
NATO	North Atlantic Treaty Organization
NBC	nuclear, biological, and chemical
NDT	nuclear disablement team
NGO	nongovernmental organization
NSF	National Strike Force (USCG)
NSPD	national security Presidential directive
NSS	national security strategy
NTRP	Navy tactical reference publication
NTTP	Navy tactics, techniques, and procedures
NWP	Navy warfare publication
OE	operational environment
OEG	operational exposure guidance
OPTEMPO	operating tempo
PIR	priority intelligence requirement
PMESII	political, military, economic, social, information, and infrastructure
PPE	personal protective equipment
RDD	radiological dispersal device
RED	radiological exposure device
RES	radiation exposure status
ROE	rules of engagement
ROM	restriction of movement
RSOI	reception, staging, onward movement, and integration
RUF	rules for the use of force
SecDef	Secretary of Defense
SJA	staff judge advocate
SME	subject matter expert
SOF	special operations forces
SPOD	seaport of debarkation
STANAG	standardization agreement (NATO)

TIB	toxic industrial biological
TIC	toxic industrial chemical
TIM	toxic industrial material
TTP	tactics, techniques, and procedures
USCG	United States Coast Guard
USG	United States Government
USSOCOM	United States Special Operations Command
USSTRATCOM	United States Strategic Command
USTRANSCOM	United States Transportation Command
VEE	Venezuelan equine encephalitis
WCE	weapons of mass destruction coordination element
WMD	weapons of mass destruction
WMD-CST	weapons of mass destruction-civil support team

acute radiation dose. Total ionizing radiation dose received at one time and over a period so short that biological recovery cannot occur. (JP 1-02. SOURCE: JP 3-11)

acute radiation syndrome. An acute illness caused by irradiation of the body by a high dose of penetrating radiation in a very short period of time. Also called **ARS.** (JP 1-02. SOURCE: JP 3-11)

atomic weapon. None. (Approved for removal from JP 1-02.)

biological agent. A microorganism (or a toxin derived from it) that causes disease in personnel, plants, or animals or causes the deterioration of materiel. (Approved for incorporation into JP 1-02.)

biological half-time. None. (Approved for removal from JP 1-02.)

biological hazard. An organism, or substance derived from an organism, that poses a threat to human or animal health. (Approved for incorporation into JP 1-02.)

biological warfare. None. (Approved for removal from JP 1-02.)

biological weapon. None. (Approved for removal from JP 1-02.)

blister agent. A chemical agent that injures the eyes and lungs, and burns or blisters the skin. Also called **vesicant agent.** (Approved for incorporation into JP 1-02.)

blood agent. A chemical compound, including the cyanide group, that affects bodily functions by preventing the normal utilization of oxygen by body tissues. (JP 1-02. SOURCE: JP 3-11)

centigray. A unit of absorbed dose of radiation (one centigray equals one rad). (JP 1-02. SOURCE: JP 3-11)

chemical agent. A chemical substance that is intended for use in military operations to kill, seriously injure, or incapacitate mainly through its physiological effects. (Approved for incorporation into JP 1-02.)

chemical, biological, radiological, and nuclear defense. Measures taken to minimize or negate the vulnerabilities to, and/or effects of, a chemical, biological, radiological, or nuclear hazard or incident. Also called **CBRN defense.** (Approved for incorporation into JP 1-02.)

chemical, biological, radiological, and nuclear environment. An operational environment that includes chemical, biological, radiological, and nuclear threats and hazards and their potential resulting effects. Also called **CBRN environment.** (Approved for incorporation into JP 1-02.)

chemical, biological, radiological, and nuclear hazard. Chemical, biological, radiological, and nuclear elements that could create adverse effects due to an accidental or deliberate release and dissemination. **Also called CBRN hazard.** (Approved for incorporation into JP 1-02.)

chemical, biological, radiological, and nuclear protection. None. (Approved for removal from JP 1-02.)

chemical, biological, radiological, and nuclear sense. None. (Approved for removal from JP 1-02.)

chemical, biological, radiological, and nuclear shape. None. (Approved for removal from JP 1-02.)

chemical, biological, radiological, and nuclear shield. None. (Approved for removal from JP 1-02.)

chemical, biological, radiological, and nuclear sustain. None. (Approved for removal from JP 1-02.)

chemical, biological, radiological, or nuclear incident. Any occurrence, resulting from the use of chemical, biological, radiological and nuclear weapons and devices; the emergence of secondary hazards arising from counterforce targeting; or the release of toxic industrial materials into the environment, involving the emergence of chemical, biological, radiological and nuclear hazards. (JP 1-02. SOURCE: JP 3-11)

chemical, biological, radiological, or nuclear weapon. A fully engineered assembly designed for employment to cause the release of a chemical or biological agent or radiological material onto a chosen target or to generate a nuclear detonation. Also called **CBRN weapon.** (JP 1-02. SOURCE: JP 3-11)

chemical hazard. Any chemical manufactured, used, transported, or stored that can cause death or other harm through toxic properties of those materials, including chemical agents and chemical weapons prohibited under the Chemical Weapons Convention as well as toxic industrial chemicals. (Approved for incorporation into JP 1-02.)

chemical warfare. All aspects of military operations involving the employment of lethal and incapacitating munitions/agents and the warning and protective measures associated with such offensive operations. Also called **CW.** (Approved for incorporation into JP 1-02.)

chemical weapon. Together or separately, (a) a toxic chemical and its precursors, except when intended for a purpose not prohibited under the Chemical Weapons Convention; (b) a munition or device, specifically designed to cause death or other harm through toxic properties of those chemicals specified in (a), above, which would be released as a result of the employment of such munition or device; (c) any equipment specifically designed for use directly in connection with the employment of munitions or devices specified in (b), above. (JP 1-02. SOURCE: JP 3-11)

clearance decontamination. The final level of decontamination that provides the decontamination of equipment and personnel to a level that allows unrestricted transportation, maintenance, employment, and disposal. (JP 1-02. SOURCE: JP 3-11)

collective protection. The protection provided to a group of individuals that permits relaxation of individual chemical, biological, radiological, and nuclear protection. Also called **COLPRO.** (Approved for incorporation into JP 1-02.)

contamination. 1. The deposit, absorption, or adsorption of radioactive material, or of biological or chemical agents on or by structures, areas, personnel, or objects. Also called **fallout radiation.** 2. Food and/or water made unfit for consumption by humans or animals because of the presence of environmental chemicals, radioactive elements, bacteria or organisms, the byproduct of the growth of bacteria or organisms, the decomposing material or waste in the food or water. (Approved for incorporation into JP 1-02.)

contamination avoidance. Individual and/or unit measures taken to reduce the effects of chemical, biological, radiological, and nuclear hazards. (JP 1-02. SOURCE: JP 3-11)

contamination control. A combination of preparatory and responsive measures designed to limit the vulnerability of forces to chemical, biological, radiological, nuclear, and toxic industrial hazards and to avoid, contain, control exposure to, and, where possible, neutralize them. (JP 1-02. SOURCE: JP 3-11)

contamination mitigation. The planning and actions taken to prepare for, respond to, and recover from contamination associated with all chemical, biological, radiological, and nuclear threats and hazards in order to continue military operations. (Approved for inclusion in JP 1-02.)

decontamination. The process of making any person, object, or area safe by absorbing, destroying, neutralizing, making harmless, or removing chemical or biological agents, or by removing radioactive material clinging to or around it. (JP 1-02. SOURCE: JP 3-11)

degree of risk. None. (Approved for removal from JP 1-02.)

deployed nuclear weapons. None. (Approved for removal from JP 1-02.)

detection. 1. In tactical operations, the perception of an object of possible military interest but unconfirmed by recognition. 2. In surveillance, the determination and transmission by a surveillance system that an event has occurred. 3. In arms control, the first step in the process of ascertaining the occurrence of a violation of an arms control agreement. 4. In chemical, biological, radiological, and nuclear environments, the act of locating chemical, biological, radiological, and nuclear hazards by use of chemical, biological, radiological, and nuclear detectors or monitoring and/or survey teams. (JP 1-02. SOURCE: JP 3-11)

half-life. The time required for the activity of a given radioactive species to decrease to half of its initial value due to radioactive decay. (Approved for incorporation into JP 1-02.)

herbicide. None. (Approved for removal from JP 1-02.)

immediate decontamination. Decontamination carried out by individuals immediately upon becoming contaminated to save lives, minimize casualties, and limit the spread of contamination. Also called **emergency decontamination.** (Approved for incorporation into JP 1-02.)

incapacitating agent. A chemical agent, which produces temporary disabling conditions that can be physical or mental and persist for hours or days after exposure to the agent has ceased. (Approved for incorporation into JP 1-02.)

individual protective equipment. In chemical, biological, radiological, or nuclear operations, the personal clothing and equipment required to protect an individual from chemical, biological, and radiological hazards and some nuclear hazards. Also called **IPE.** (JP 1-02. SOURCE: JP 3-11)

initial radiation. The radiation, essentially neutrons and gamma rays, resulting from a nuclear burst and emitted from the fireball within one minute after burst. (JP 1-02. SOURCE: JP 3-11)

ionizing radiation. Particulate (alpha, beta, and neutron) and electromagnetic (X-ray and gamma) radiation of sufficient energy to displace electrons from atoms, producing ions. (JP 1-02. SOURCE: JP 3-11)

mission-oriented protective posture. A flexible system of protection against chemical, biological, radiological, and nuclear contamination in which personnel are required to wear only that protective clothing and equipment appropriate to the threat level, work rate imposed by the mission, temperature, and humidity. Also called **MOPP.** (Approved for incorporation into JP 1-02.)

mission-oriented protective posture gear. Military term for individual protective equipment including suit, boots, gloves, mask with hood, first aid treatments, and decontamination kits issued to military members. Also called **MOPP gear.** (JP 1-02. SOURCE: JP 3-11)

nerve agent. A potentially lethal chemical agent that interferes with the transmission of nerve impulses. (Approved for incorporation into JP 1-02.)

nonpersistent agent. A chemical agent that when released dissipates and/or loses its ability to cause casualties after 10 to 15 minutes. (JP 1-02. SOURCE: JP 3-11)

nuclear radiation. None. (Approved for removal from JP 1-02.)

nuclear weapon. None. (Approved for removal from JP 1-02.)

operational decontamination. Decontamination carried out by an individual and/or a unit, restricted to specific parts of operationally essential equipment, materiel and/or working areas, in order to minimize contact and transfer hazards and to sustain operations. (Approved for incorporation into JP 1-02.)

operational exposure guidance. The maximum amount of nuclear/external ionizing radiation that the commander considers a unit may be permitted to receive while performing a particular mission or missions. Also called **OEG.** (Approved for replacement of "operational exposure guide" in JP 1-02.)

overpressure. The pressure resulting from the blast wave of an explosion referred to as "positive" when it exceeds atmospheric pressure and "negative" during the passage of the wave when resulting pressures are less than atmospheric pressure. (Approved for incorporation into JP 1-02.)

pathogen. None. (Approved for removal from JP 1-02.)

persistency. None. (Approved for removal from JP 1-02.)

persistent agent. A chemical agent that, when released, remains able to cause casualties for more than 24 hours to several days or weeks. (JP 1-02. SOURCE: JP 3-11)

personal protective equipment. The protective clothing and equipment provided to shield or isolate a person from the chemical, physical, and thermal hazards that can be encountered at a hazardous materials incident. Also called **PPE.** (Approved for incorporation into JP 1-02.)

precursor. None. (Approved for removal from JP 1-02.)

protective clothing. Clothing especially designed, fabricated, or treated to protect personnel against hazards. (Approved for incorporation into JP 1-02.)

protective mask. None. (Approved for removal from JP 1-02.)

radiation dose. The total amount of ionizing radiation absorbed by material or tissues. (JP 1-02. SOURCE: JP 3-11)

radiation dose rate. Measurement of radiation dose per unit of time. (JP 1-02. SOURCE: JP 3-11)

radiation exposure status. Criteria to assist the commander in measuring unit exposure to radiation based on total past cumulative dose, normally expressed in centigray. Also called **RES.** (JP 1-02. SOURCE: JP 3-11)

radiological dispersal device. An improvised assembly or process, other than a nuclear explosive device, designed to disseminate radioactive material in order to cause destruction, damage, or injury. Also called **RDD.** (JP 1-02. SOURCE: JP 3-11)

radiological exposure device. A radioactive source placed to cause injury or death. Also called **RED.** (JP 1-02. SOURCE: JP 3-11)

residual radiation. Nuclear radiation caused by fallout, artificial dispersion of radioactive material, or irradiation that results from a nuclear explosion and persists longer than one minute after burst. (Approved for incorporation into JP 1-02.)

riot control agent. Any chemical, not listed in a schedule of the Convention on the Prohibition of the Development, Production, Stockpiling and Use of Chemical Weapons and on their Destruction that can produce rapidly in humans sensory irritation or disabling physical effects that disappear within a short time following termination of exposure. Also called **RCA.** (Approved for incorporation into JP 1-02.)

shielding. 1. Material of suitable thickness and physical characteristics used to protect personnel from radiation during the manufacture, handling, and transportation of fissionable and radioactive materials. 2. Obstructions that tend to protect personnel or materials from the effects of a nuclear explosion. (Approved for incorporation into JP 1-02.)

split-mission oriented protective posture. The concept of maintaining heightened protective posture only in those areas (or zones) that are contaminated, allowing personnel in uncontaminated areas to continue to operate in a reduced posture. Also called **split-MOPP.** (JP 1-02. SOURCE: JP 3-11)

thorough decontamination. Decontamination carried out by a unit to reduce contamination on personnel, equipment, materiel, and/or working areas equal to natural background or to the lowest possible levels, to permit the partial or total removal of individual protective equipment and to maintain operations with minimum degradation. (Approved for incorporation into JP 1-02.)

toxic industrial biological. Any biological material manufactured, used, transported, or stored by industrial, medical, or commercial processes which could pose an infectious or toxic threat. Also called **TIB.** (JP 1-02. SOURCE: JP 3-11)

toxic industrial chemical. A chemical developed or manufactured for use in industrial operations or research by industry, government, or academia that poses a hazard. Also called **TIC.** (Approved for incorporation into JP 1-02.)

toxic industrial material. A generic term for toxic, chemical, biological, or radioactive substances in solid, liquid, aerosolized, or gaseous form that may be used, or stored for use, for industrial, commercial, medical, military, or domestic purposes. Also called **TIM.** (Approved for incorporation into JP 1-02.)

toxic industrial radiological. Any radiological material manufactured, used, transported, or stored by industrial, medical, or commercial processes. Also called **TIR.** (Approved for incorporation into JP 1-02.)

toxin. None. (Approved for removal from JP 1-02.)

vesicant agent. None. (Approved for removal from JP 1-02.)

Intentionally Blank

JOINT DOCTRINE PUBLICATIONS HIERARCHY

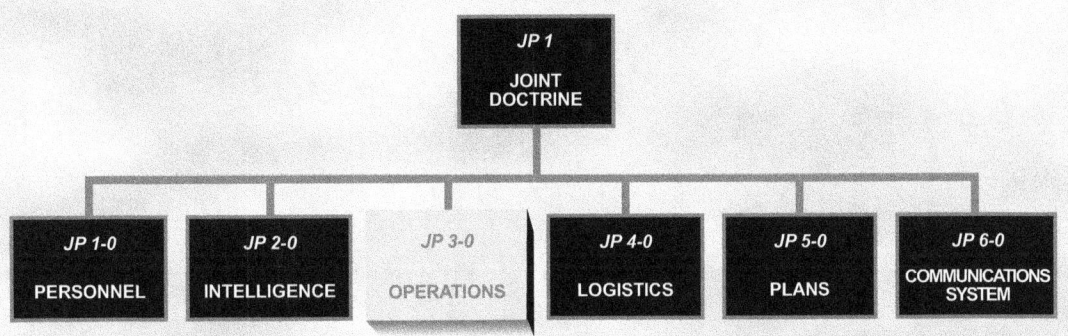

JP 1 JOINT DOCTRINE					
JP 1-0 PERSONNEL	JP 2-0 INTELLIGENCE	JP 3-0 OPERATIONS	JP 4-0 LOGISTICS	JP 5-0 PLANS	JP 6-0 COMMUNICATIONS SYSTEM

All joint publications are organized into a comprehensive hierarchy as shown in the chart above. **Joint Publication (JP) 3-11** is in the **Operations** series of joint doctrine publications. The diagram below illustrates an overview of the development process:

STEP #4 - Maintenance

- JP published and continuously assessed by users
- Formal assessment begins 24 27 months following publication
- Revision begins 3.5 years after publication
- Each JP revision is completed no later than 5 years after signature

STEP #1 - Initiation

- Joint doctrine development community (JDDC) submission to fill extant operational void
- Joint Staff (JS) J 7 conducts front end analysis
- Joint Doctrine Planning Conference validation
- Program directive (PD) development and staffing/joint working group
- PD includes scope, references, outline, milestones, and draft authorship
- JS J 7 approves and releases PD to lead agent (LA) (Service, combatant command, JS directorate)

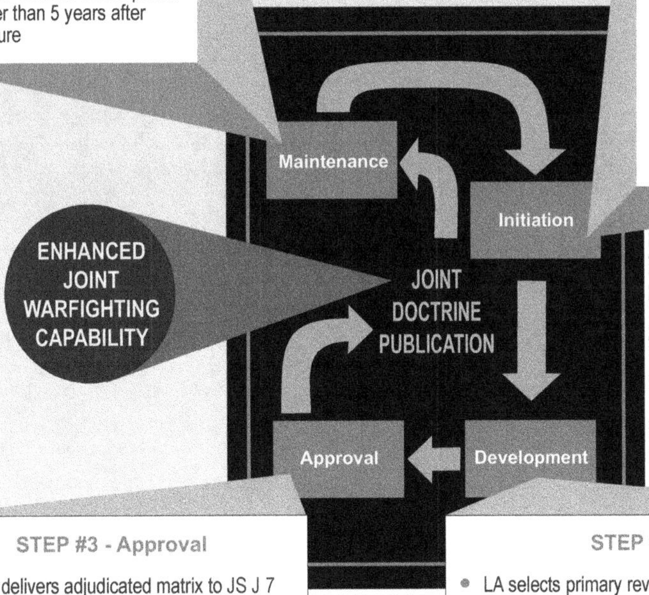

ENHANCED JOINT WARFIGHTING CAPABILITY

Maintenance

Initiation

JOINT DOCTRINE PUBLICATION

Approval

Development

STEP #3 - Approval

- JSDS delivers adjudicated matrix to JS J 7
- JS J 7 prepares publication for signature
- JSDS prepares JS staffing package
- JSDS staffs the publication via JSAP for signature

STEP #2 - Development

- LA selects primary review authority (PRA) to develop the first draft (FD)
- PRA develops FD for staffing with JDDC
- FD comment matrix adjudication
- JS J 7 produces the final coordination (FC) draft, staffs to JDDC and JS via Joint Staff Action Processing (JSAP) system
- Joint Staff doctrine sponsor (JSDS) adjudicates FC comment matrix
- FC joint working group